PRAISE FOR ASHA ARAVINDAKSHAN'S
SKILLS: THE COMMON DENOMINATOR

"Through the stories in *Skills*—both of others' career journeys and her own—Asha Aravindakshan thoughtfully presents a framework for packaging one's skills to enter new roles. Her narratives are relatable and varied, with tidbits to learn from hidden on every page."

—Amelia DeSorrento, *Forbes 30* Under 30

"Asha Aravindakshan does a great job of bringing together stories of change in *Skills*. If you want to make a big pivot in your career, this book will give you hope that it's possible."

—Angela Guido, Founder of Career Protocol and FriendMo and Bestselling Author of *Interview Hero: How to Ace Your Interviews, Find Your Voice,* and *Direct the Narrative of Your Life*

"In *Skills*, Asha Aravindakshan tells story after story of people who figured out how to identify their transferable skills, how to package those skills for their prospective next employer, and then how they landed the job in a new field. From these real-world examples, she extracts valuable principles that will be helpful to anyone—in any stage of their career—who is contemplating working in a new field. This is genuinely useful information."

—Bob Jones, CEO of Scientific Nutrition Products, National Advisor of Pipeline Entrepreneurs, and Lecturer, MIT Nuts and Bolts of New Ventures

"Asha Aravindakshan delivers a structured approach for individuals to determine their strengths and apply that understanding to their professional journeys."

—Chip Conley, Founder of Modern Elder Academy

"Asha Aravindakshan and the vignettes presented in *Skills* provide sound, experience-based mentorship for anyone seeking to maximize their potential in the workplace. Highlighting the themes of hard work, persistence, dedication, and problem-solving, this book underscores the non-technical skills that are always—and will always be—valued in the workplace."

—David Gragan, Chief Learning Officer
of DC Government and former Chief Procurement
Officer for the States of Texas and Indiana

"Asha Aravindakshan's *Skills* is the essential employment guide for the decade."

—Devin Thorpe, Author of *Superpowers
for Good* and *Adding Profit by Adding Purpose*

"*Skills* is a great and informative read, well written with very relatable examples and situations. Included a lot of innovative ideas on expanding business networks that I cannot wait to put into practice, well done!"

—Donna Day, Director of People at SkyKick

"Asha Aravindakshan's *Skills: The Common Denominator* presents the modern approach to using preparation, technology, and social capital to build a career and opportunity sustaining network. Asha invites each reader to reflect on the inherent value of their respective journey."

—Joe Scantlebury, Incoming President &
CEO of Living Cities

"This book is an informative, supportive and tactical guide to identifying and using transferable skills for lifelong career success. Asha Aravindakshan's personal stories and the many real-life examples she includes bring the content to life and make it relatable to people from a wide variety of backgrounds and career interests. Highly recommended for anyone considering a career pivot!"

—Lindsey Pollak, *The New York Times* bestselling author of *Becoming the Boss, The Remix, and Recalculating*

"Practical steps through engaging, real-life stories. Researched-based content—like reading Cliff Notes—led me to see *Skills* as a valuable tool I can go to again and again."

—Moira Lethbridge, Author of *Savvy Woman in 5 Minutes a Day: Make Time for a Life That Matters*

"Asha presents an informative, engaging, and digestible series of real-life stories. They all clearly demonstrate the importance of continually investing in transferable skills as you build your career. She encourages us all to go for it, and reminds us that the power and skill to do so is right at our fingertips."

—Mubuso Zamchiya, Founder of Zamchiya Books and Rhodes Scholar

"With thoughtful examples from various sectors, *Skills* provides a roadmap with various routes to help both young professionals and folks looking to transition careers. The tangible anecdotes give a variety of experiences allowing more seasoned readers the ability to connect the dots within their own career, making it easier to translate their experience to colleagues looking for career advice and recommendations."

—Naomi Shelton, CEO of National Charter Collaborative

"Using her own and others experiences as examples, Asha Aravindakshan shows us how to use the skills we've developed to move into new opportunities. *Skills* is a must read for anyone looking to change their career focus in a post pandemic world."

—Natalya Bah, Coauthor of *The Power of Perspective*

"Asha Aravindakshan shares invaluable insights from her own personal experience and profiles of others on career planning and transition including understanding and building your transferable skills, finding your passion and how to market yourself for new opportunities. Career paths are oftentimes nonlinear and thoughtful pivots are necessary. *Skills* explains how to embrace uncertainty, change and converting that into your success."

—Peter Callstrom, President and CEO
of the San Diego Workforce Partnership

"Pivots at work, fueled by personal skills, are the new career currency. By sharing personal stories of individuals' skills based on what they do and not where they do it, Asha Aravindakshan provides both powerful and liberating insights. The lesson? For true success and impact, embrace a career that embraces your skills…"

—Ron Reed, Founder and Executive Producer of SXSW EDU

"Asha Aravindakshan nails a key point about professional development in *Skills*. We develop skills in each role, often without realizing it. Oftentimes we need other people to show us that we have proven a mastery of skills that we never realized we had."

—Sameer Acharya, Communications and Social Media
Consultant and Author of *Saraswatichandra*

"As our lives become exponentially non-linear, it is imperative we learn to embrace and not resist career transitions. *Skills* is timely and spot on. Not only have I personally leveraged the principals of transferable skills, connecting the dots and utilizing my network, it's what I hear my podcast guests share when they describe their career transition journeys. As an entrepreneur, I live by plans A, B and Z!"

—Sonali Batish, President of Cospan Consulting
and Host of *My 2.0* Podcast

"A fluid read that truly bends one's thinking about career paths. I've often watched hiring in my profession become laser focused on prior job titles and parallel past responsibilities. But the stories in *Skills* demonstrate that successful applicants flower for reasons that go well beyond directly applicable experience. Asha Aravindakshan reveals how passion, imagination, and adapted skills contain the real secret of professional potential."

—Torey Malatia, President, CEO and
General Manager of The Public's Radio 89.3FM

"A compelling read that shares easy-to-use frameworks and brings them to life with real-life case studies. I highly recommend *Skills* for anyone facing a future career pivot—whether planned or unplanned."

—Victor Prince, Former COO of the Consumer
Financial Protection Bureau and Author
of *The Camino Way* and *Lead Inside the Box*

"*Skills* is a must read for young people, job hunters of all ages, and anyone interested in the future of work. The author, a skillful storyteller, brilliantly describes specific paths to new careers taken by everyday people. As an educator turned technology entrepreneur, I found myself nodding all the way from beginning to end."

—Ximena Hartsock, Cofounder of BuildWithin Inc.

SKILLS:
THE COMMON DENOMINATOR

SKILLS: THE COMMON DENOMINATOR

ASHA ARAVINDAKSHAN

NEW DEGREE PRESS

COPYRIGHT © 2021 ASHA ARAVINDAKSHAN

SKILLS: THE COMMON DENOMINATOR

ISBN   978-1-63676-383-5   *Paperback*
        978-1-63676-453-5   *Kindle Ebook*
        978-1-63676-384-2   *Ebook*

To Mom & Dad,

Bona fide career pivoters.

TABLE OF CONTENTS

──────

I shall either find a way or make one.

—HANNIBAL BARCA

INTRODUCTION

———

On a bright, sunny Saturday morning in late September 2013, I walked to the George Washington University (GW) student union as a volunteer for an alumni weekend event, "Managing a Successful Career." Max Fira sat down at my table, with another alumna, both with resumes in hand. Until a month before this event, Fira worked at a local event production company, so her resume resembled mine at a similar age. She completed three years at the organization, having worked on their annual event, coordinated with sponsors and vendors, and produced marketing collateral. She described a number of reasons for her departure a month prior, including "the culture and opportunity for growth was not there."

Now, Fira wanted to pivot towards a career in management consulting, which was more structured and supportive from a professional growth perspective. From conversations with friends that were management consultants, she observed, "Right out of school, they were doing research and presenting it to C-level executives. In that role, you are able to deliver value to help companies to make better decisions." She also found the field compelling because "these [local firms] were global companies, so [she] knew that [she] would have the opportunity to move around the US and perhaps, abroad."

As we talked, I explained to Fira her relationship management work with sponsors and vendors could transfer to client work in consulting. I could see the feedback resonated with Fira as she realized she had the necessary skills to switch industries and did not need to start her career over. However, she needed to rewrite her resume bullets using the STAR (situation/task, action, and result) method and quantify the results to make them sound more business oriented so recruiters would be able to spot those transferable skills more easily. I offered to review her resume again and provide an alumni referral for her with my former employer, the Corporate Executive Board (CEB, now Gartner). Fira followed up by email on Monday. Then we worked on her resume and LinkedIn profile by email over the next few weeks before I submitted it for a few relevant openings.

Fira started the interview process at CEB and contacted me to prepare for each round of interviews. She also found two current employees to ask about the culture to make sure it lined up with her online research. She became drawn to the firm for their corporate social responsibility initiatives. By the new year, Fira received a full-time offer in the sales and service professional development program at Level 2, which recognized the skills she gained from her previous employment. She thrived in her new setting and is celebrating eight years in progressive roles with the company at the time of this writing.

How was I able to connect the dots in Fira's situation? Because CEB recognized my transferable skills a decade earlier.

Six months after my college graduation, I needed to find a more stable career. I joined a nonprofit organization at the height of the technology boom in May 2000, but its funding was on a downward slope. The monthly open bar events I organized for a thousand local technology executives at The Ritz-Carlton, Tyson's Corner were converted into quarterly cash bar affairs for a few hundred professionals at the Hilton McLean across the street. My passion for event planning had run its course.

In this moment, I knew something needed to change. I decided to focus on finding a role in a corporate environment, leveraging my skills from my years of college internships and nonprofit work. I reached out to my friends and professional contacts to let them know I was on a job hunt.

I reached out to one of the directors on the nonprofit's board about an accounting position at his firm that aligned with my business studies, and he suggested that I try sales instead. After interviewing with the sales team, I realized I was not interested in the amount of cold calling required for an entry-level sales position.

At the same time, Mital Desai, who I met through GW student life, shared that his older sister, Shejal, enjoyed working at CEB and he could also see me working there. She referred me and after a set of interviews, I received an offer for an analyst role on the newly-formed strategic accounts team. My new managers commented that because I had a year of full-time professional experience, I stood out from the other candidates. Unbeknownst to us, the skills I gained in event planning transferred nicely to account management. In this new role, we worked backward from the customer's renewal date to ensure successful service delivery, which was similar to how I set up an event plan in advance of an actual event date.

Through this experience (and the many others that followed), I saw that others could connect the dots on my skills in ways I could not imagine. I also saw how referrals could open doors into my target firms. So, when I met Fira, I paid it forward by demonstrating the relevance of her current skill set, expanding her list of potential employers, and providing a warm referral to my prior employer.

In today's world, employers fixate on job titles and inherent experience within the same industry. Employers, recruiters, and hiring managers should focus on the skills they need to augment their teams and which job candidates have those skills, even if they come from a different sector or functional area. Both Fira and I benefited from this open-mindedness with the same company as we pivoted roles from event planning to account management nearly a decade apart.

Could others leverage their professional networks to make similar pivots, harnessing their transferable skills? Based on my job search experiences and the hundreds I informally advised over the years, it is possible.

CAREER PIVOTS ARE TRENDING

According to Indeed's 2019 "Career Change" survey of 662 full-time employees at various US companies, nearly half (49 percent) made a dramatic career shift while 65 percent of the others thought or were thinking about it. Indeed defined a dramatic career shift as a total career change, for example, from marketing to engineering or from teaching to finance. The top reasons for changing careers included job satisfaction, growth, pay, and work/life balance.

Indeed 2019 Career Change Survey

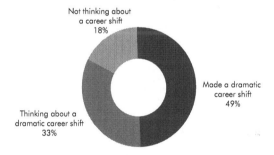

Not thinking about a career shift 18%

Thinking about a dramatic career shift 33%

Made a dramatic career shift 49%

An important insight from the Indeed survey was that those dramatic career shifts take an average of eleven months. This is typically not an overnight decision, but one made with careful deliberation. The significantly high percentages in the "why do workers change careers?" section indicated how a combination of these top five factors lend to an individual deciding to make a dramatic career shift:

- Were unhappy in a previous job/sector
- Wanted greater flexibility

- Wanted to earn more money
- Did not feel challenged or satisfied
- Wanted more opportunities for advancement

Finally, of those 49 percent of US workers that made a dramatic shift, 88 percent are happier with their decision.

In an April 2018 interview on CNBC *Make It*, Stacey Morgenstern, cofounder of the Health Coach Institute, validated that career fulfillment through pay, work/life balance, and recognition are major factors for a dramatic career shift. She recommended people consider what they enjoy in their free time and understand whether that can be translated into a career, by saying, "Notice what you are fascinated by and want to talk about all the time. Notice what people naturally come to you for." When I was in college, I sought to explore my personal interests in politics and event planning through summer internships. I enjoyed the event planning internship so much that it became my first full-time job after graduation.

SHOULD I STAY OR SHOULD I GO?

When Daniel H. Pink published *Drive: The Surprising Truth about What Motivates Us* in December 2009, my then manager, Bryan Sivak, the chief technology officer of the Government of the District of Columbia, required his leadership team to read the book. Pink's key finding showed that if an employer tried to motivate employees with incentives for completing certain types of work ("carrot and stick incentives"), in their quest for the incentives, employees lose the enjoyment of learning or problem solving. This counterintuitive finding explains why those individuals that turn a passion into full-time employment to earn more money end up losing their passion for the hobby.

One solution for this behavior that employers could offer is to amplify the intrinsic drivers of an employee's motivation, as Pink recommends, through autonomy, mastery, and purpose.

Pink's message also served as a beacon on how we as individuals can ensure we find fulfillment in our careers.

- Autonomy serves as a prompt to keep yourself in the driver's seat of your career and its path
- Mastery highlights the need to focus on strengthening our skills that bring us joy
- Purpose reminds us of why we do what we do and who we do it for

With constant career reinvention becoming the new normal, we need to think of ourselves in permanent beta. We are a work in progress and never a finished product. Reid Hoffman and Ben Casnocha outline this concept in their 2012 book, *The Start-up of You*. Their recommendation is to look at the key things we do to manage our careers in the modern world and learn how to adaptively plan for our careers.

- Plan A: what you're doing right now
- Plan B: possible pivots
- Plan Z: a reset option (or fallback) when Plans A and B do not go in the direction you want

In Part I, these stories I share have a common thread—skills you demonstrate in your job, volunteer activities, classes, or entrepreneurial pursuits are visible to those around you. Your skills are memorable to others. These transferable skills are what matter in today's economy. When you embark on conversations related to a job search or career change, skill-based networking is critical. Your professional networks will provide anecdotal feedback on your candidacy for a role based on those moments where your skills stood out to them.

HOLD MY HAND

Skill-based networking can create a nonlinear career path because your skills may not always align to a traditional role or may lead to a role created for you.

You can't connect the dots looking forward; you can only connect them looking backwards. So you have to trust that the dots will somehow connect in your future. You have to trust in something—your gut, destiny, life, karma, whatever.

—STEVE JOBS, STANFORD UNIVERSITY
2005 COMMENCEMENT ADDRESS.

My professional journey has been anything but linear, defined by several unplanned major career pivots:

- Sector—from the nonprofit sector to private sector to public sector in the first ten years of my career
- Functional area—from strategy to marketing to finance to human resources in the next ten years of my career
- Role type—from consultant to full-time employee in the same organization (twice)

- Location—from Washington, DC, to New York, NY, to Cambridge, MA, to Buenos Aires, Argentina, to New York, NY

Through all the changes I experienced, there were several constants that defined them:

- My demonstrated skills left an impression on a future manager or referral.
- I joined each organization to solve a particular problem via referral.
- I did not have a history in that particular sector or functional area.

And in some of these cases, such as the Indeed survey participants, I chose to make a career shift before the opportunity arrived at my doorstep. During those windows of time, I dedicated myself wholeheartedly to the job hunt by crafting a narrative on my transferable skills, learning about online applications the hard way, and leveraging digital tools to broaden my search. In Part II, I share these systematic techniques with examples to accelerate your pivot to a career that embraces your skills.

From the day we start our careers until retirement, we can find ourselves in a constant search of what is next. In writing this book, I aim to help:

- High school and university students approaching graduation
- Recent college graduates still building their careers

- Professionals looking to make that switch into a new career

We—both the employers and the job candidates—need to stretch our thinking outside of what is written in a job description to see what is necessary for a role and who can satisfy those requirements. In this sense, those that believe that job specialization is the key to success should start to look at the generalists as capable of meeting the job demands in today's economy.

Be ready for your next career pivot by reading this book to learn real-life stories of people that made pivots in their industry or functional area, how transferable skills can help you to grow an illustrious career, and tried-and-true methods for a successful job hunt.

In our new normal, your transferable skills give you a competitive advantage. I'll empower you to discover that next opportunity. Let's go!

PART I

SKILLS ILLUSTRATED

CHAPTER ONE

ASHA ARAVINDAKSHAN: MY STORY

———

"Three quarters of American college graduates go onto a career unrelated to their major," wrote David Epstein in his best-selling book, *Range*. I fell into this statistic; I majored in finance, with the intention to pursue a Wall Street job in investment banking. With limited opportunities for on-campus recruiting interviews in fall 2001, I eagerly accepted an offer to turn my event planning internship into a newly-created, full-time operations manager role, with expanded responsibilities. None of our business curriculum focused on the day-to-day aspects of running a small business, so I taught myself.

In his book, Epstein showcased The Dark Horse Project at the Harvard Graduate School of Education, a long-term study of how women and men achieve success by harnessing their individuality. He highlighted how the study subjects "sampled many different roles, in many different fields, and worked with a variety of people." The study's researchers concluded the commonality of the most successful participants was their mindset:

Here's who I am at this moment, here are my motivations, here's what I've found I like to do, here's what I'd like to learn, and here are the opportunities. Which opportunity is the best match right now?

Epstein's own conclusion from the research: "It's clear from the science that our work preferences and our life preferences do not stay the same because we do not stay the same." He explained that the "only way to have a good career fit is to have a wide range of experiences, sampling different jobs, and experimenting with different ideas. The more time we take early on in our career to have a wide range of experiences, interact with a wide range of people, the more analogies that we will accumulate, which will allow us to solve more and more nuanced problems and be more effective in any career we eventually commit to."

In my first job, I learned I could dabble in different business areas, including board meeting preparation, corporate branding and payroll, learning the ins and outs, connecting the dots between the company's initiatives, and ultimately, shaping the outcomes to benefit the organization. That choice helped me to maintain a generalist approach to my career. In subsequent roles, I entered as a generalist, then did deep dives to emerge as a specialist.

Read on to understand how I was able to pursue a variety of career experiences to develop my transferable skills. Pay special attention to the personal and professional contacts that opened the door for me to those opportunities. The first part of the book explores that intersection of transferable skills and professional networks through fourteen stories, starting with mine.

MY JOURNEY

Growing up in Brooklyn, NY, I watched both of my parents switch from the private sector to the public sector in their careers. When I graduated from Elmont Memorial High School, I chose to attend The George Washington University (GW), blocks away from the White House. In Washington, DC, we are lucky to be situated at the intersection of politics, business, and nongovernmental organizations. These organizations provided ample opportunity to gain professional experience during our academic pursuits, so much so that at GW, Peter Konwerski, the former dean of student affairs, coined the phrase, "At GW, internships are our football."

My academic journey was fulfilling as it included academics, student life, internships, and entrepreneurship. Some students chose to focus on school and others found it difficult to balance school with extracurriculars, but I thrived on a packed schedule. I also sought to integrate my scholastic interests with my personal interests.

I was diligent about what experiences I wanted to have as a student before completing my undergraduate degree, including:

- Securing an internship with a financial services company through Laveen Venugopalan, a family friend with the same major, who was a year ahead of me in school;

- Negotiating a Congressional internship in a conference call, with the help of David Nurnberg, my next-door neighbor in the Thurston Hall freshman dorm;
- Taking over a part-time customer service role at a doctor's office, after Sinu Kurian, my freshman year roommate, decided to transfer our sophomore year;
- Channeling my passion for event planning into multiple opportunities—an entrepreneurial venture, a summer internship, and a volunteer role with a young professional's organization.

I secured every single one of these experiences through referrals from my GW classmates and friends. Without them, it was not possible. All of these referrals were within one degree—my roommate, my neighbor, and students in other classes. The important skill is to vocalize what you are searching for, with specificity.

My summer internship that started in May 2000 evolved into my first full-time role in January 2002. After a year of working full-time and a total of three years with the entrepreneurial association, The IndUS Entrepreneurs, Washington, DC Chapter (TiE DC), I moved into a private sector role at CEB. I enjoyed my time at CEB, being promoted into progressive roles, and I imagined working there forever.

Then, in late March 2007, I stepped outside of the CEB office on K Street to walk home, when I got a phone call from Vivek Kundra, a contact I met through TiE DC asking me to join the new mayoral administration. Earlier in the day, Mayor Adrian Fenty appointed Kundra to the role of chief technology officer on his mayoral cabinet, and now, he declared,

"I am building my team and I want you to be part of it." I always wanted to work in politics—remember that Capitol Hill internship?—and jumped at the chance. Although seven years had passed since I first met him, I left a positive impression that warranted this opportunity. We worked closely together for almost two years, so when Kundra called me again about a role on his new team at Sprinklr in summer 2018, I felt it was a no-brainer to work with him again.

I worked for four years in the Government of the District of Columbia, the seat of local government for the nation's capital, and loved my role as chief of staff of the Office of the Chief Technology Officer (OCTO). I did it so well that every quarter at the periodic gathering of the seventy to eighty chiefs of staff across the government, Neil Albert, the city administrator, would highlight one of my initiatives as a best practice the others could learn from. My innate ability coupled with this regular recognition triggered my desire to serve in the equivalent role of chief operations officer (COO) in a private company.

When Mayor Fenty lost reelection in fall 2010, I was not sure what to do next or where to start for the new year. I ordered personal business cards and for thirty days, I planned lunches and coffees with interesting people in my personal and professional networks. I would explain:

- What I did,
- What skills I had, and
- Asked how I could fit into their organizations.

My spin on an informational interview helped me decipher my transferable skills and learn the range of job titles that existed to align to them. Through these conversations, I was able to connect the dots that event planning (which I learned at TiE DC and from running my own events firm), account management (which I learned at CEB), and project management (which I learned at OCTO) were similar in nature, with customer service as the underlying ethos.

During this time, I also shared my job hunt with my closest friends. Nurnberg worked for Civic Entertainment Group, an experiential marketing agency started by a GW alumnus in New York City. He invited me to visit him at his Park Avenue office and meet his colleagues in February 2011. I ended up having unplanned informal interviews with three executives during the visit. It is important to always be prepared! A couple of months later, some team members unexpectedly resigned, so they called me on a Tuesday in late April saying they needed a project manager to start right away. I thought "why not?" and joined Civic that weekend on the road in Chicago, supporting their client, NBC News. I enjoyed working with the team for six months but learned I did not like the small company environment.

While I worked at Civic, Joe Walsh, a former colleague from the DC Government, stayed in touch during his job search. That summer, he joined the Bill & Melinda Gates Foundation, which was a sponsor of the Education Nation summit I worked on for NBC News. A few months later, he reached out to me about a portfolio manager role on his team. We worked together on two two-week projects during his tenure—so a short time—but again, I left a positive impression that made

Walsh think of me for the role. At first, I was not sure if this role was right for me, but after he sent a customized job description in his third outreach with the note "I think your skill set could knock it out of the park if interested," I realized it would leverage my account management skills, coupled with the strategy and budgeting skills I learned while at OCTO. When we explored the two potential hiring paths as a consultant or full-time employee, Walsh explained that I could start as a consultant within two weeks, but a full-time employee role would take several months, so we settled on a consulting role that began at the end of February 2012. While I enjoyed the challenge of figuring out the world of philanthropy, I learned I did not like the office culture, so I was ready for a change in 2013.

INFLECTION POINT

On January 1, 2013, I posted my new year's resolution on Facebook—I wanted to be a step closer to the COO role I set forth as my intention a few years earlier. Knowing that role may not be familiar to my personal friends, I wrote that I wanted "to oversee the administrative functions in a startup environment." Being vulnerable about my job search was uncomfortable, but I knew it was the best way to surface information I would not find on my own. My post received a few responses from GW alumni, including a lead to meet a venture capitalist that had recently relocated from San Francisco to the DC area. Today, you can post on multiple social media platforms that you are graduating or seeking full-time employment to throw your search wide open. Remember to be as specific as possible with the type of industry, role, organization, and city, so your network knows how to help you.

A few weeks later, I remember sitting on the couch on a Saturday afternoon thinking about my skills and gaps toward becoming a COO of a growing organization. I reasoned that while I had strong skills in strategy, performance management, budgeting, technology, account/portfolio management, and business operations, I should take deeper dives into human resources and marketing to be well rounded. According to Anna Phan's thesis research, I was a "targeted searcher" concerned with finding the skills to make a nonlinear transition possible.

I pressed myself a bit more when I asked myself, "What do you want to do?" Then, I surprised myself by saying out loud, "I want to change the world." I am not one to talk to myself, so the action and statement caught me off guard, but it felt right. A few hours later, I scrolled through my Twitter feed and stumbled upon a *Forbes* article called "How to change the world and still pay your bills." Written by Emily Bosland, she described recently completing her master's in business administration (MBA) and changing organizations from the inside as an "intrapraneur." While I did not have an MBA, I had an undergraduate business degree and I changed companies from the inside, so as Bosland described, I was an intrapraneur too.

As I wrote this book, I had the chance to speak with Bosland about her motivation to write this article. Bosland grew up in New Mexico raised by academics who embraced public service. After graduating from college in spring 2003, she described, "It was important to participate in AmeriCorps," which is a service fellowship. Hers was funded by IBM, which exposed her to how much influence the corporation had in her community. IBM hired Bosland to evolve her fellowship program into a public-private partnership in 2007, which gave her an insider's view of how they can affect social change policy through grants and community initiatives. The balance of power that rested with IBM in these corporate social responsibility relationships colored her decision to pursue an MBA at the University of Colorado Boulder. "Business was going to change the world," she repeated to me more than once in our conversation.

Following the completion of her MBA in spring 2010, she joined the Ashoka Changemakers team in Washington, DC, as a senior manager to work together with corporations and nongovernmental organizations on social change initiatives. She described one of her projects enforced "the idea that everyone can be an agent for social change, whether as an entrepreneur or an intrapraneur," which supported Ashoka's "everyone a changemaker" mantra. Bosland reflected that she "found the topic of intrapraneurship really interesting," so she "volunteered to write an article about it as part of the Ashoka-Forbes partnership" that synthesized her findings from this project. She added a personal angle to the story by layering in her MBA experience.

I spent the next few hours researching the organizations listed in Bosland's article, as they supported intrapraneurs, and also researched her employer, Ashoka: Innovators for the Public. Founded by Bill Drayton, a now forty-one-year-old nonprofit pioneered social entrepreneurship, located in

Rosslyn, VA, across the Potomac River from where I lived in DC. Its values of empathy, teamwork, and leadership strongly resonated with me, so I scoured the web looking for their current job openings. Their own website did not have a job board, but a generic job application. An internet search led me to a job description for a role on the human resources team called the director of talent operations, but with no place to apply. I returned to the generic web application on the Ashoka website and submitted my resume, with my fingers crossed they would consider me for the role.

During this time, I loaded my daily schedule with job hunt activities, volunteering, attending networking events, exercising at a gym, and taking online classes. I signed up for a class from the Acumen Academy with a flipped learning model, where we reviewed the coursework online, then participated in a local meet-up group to discuss the materials. In the meet-up group, I met Marcia Call, a recruiter for local technology companies. We hit it off right away because we found contacts in common, a shared interest in education, and appreciated the class discussions.

A few weeks after we wrapped up our class, Call invited me to the Smithsonian for an event honoring Drayton. After the event, we stepped out of the auditorium, where she told me she started pro bono recruiting for Ashoka and there was a role she wanted me to consider. I interrupted her and said, "Let me guess—it's the director of talent operations?"

Call was shocked and asked, "How did you know that?"

I shared that I applied for the same role online a few months prior, but never heard back. She promised to get my resume in front of the hiring manager. In turn, I had two other extensive interview processes underway for roles that came through referrals, but they did not feel like the right fit, so I declined the offers to wait for an interview process to start with Ashoka. It started six weeks later, leading to nine interviews. Eight months after setting the intention to work at Ashoka as the director of talent operations, I started in the role at the end of September 2013.

I spent two and a half years at Ashoka, where the common refrain was, "Asha's building the plane while flying it." Without a background in human resources, I relied on my prior experiences as an employee and manager in different organizations to envision how the talent operations team should serve the organization's 450 employees spread out across forty-seven countries. My approach resulted in building multiple award-winning programs during the first year of my tenure. It also made me realize I wanted to work in an environment where more people moved at my speed.

On a Tuesday evening in August 2014, I attended the Forté Foundation MBA Forum for Women at the Omni Shoreham Hotel. Forté is an organization that came onto my radar a few years prior for its programming targeted to women considering an MBA. I referred others to it for years; now, I would see if I should take part in it. The evening's first panel featured alumni of business schools reflecting on how their academic experiences brought them competence, confidence, and credibility. When I reviewed my notes from that event, their statements that resonate with me now (as they did then) included:

- The value of the degree is in its credibility—others know you have skills; you know you have the skills to do the job
- Establish classroom competence—be your authentic self; be collaborative within the team space
- For those pursuing a non-traditional path, the MBA provides business skills that can be used in any environment

That evening cemented my decision to pursue my MBA, with the guidance of the Forté MBA Launch program. I spent the next few months mentally preparing for the decision to leave the workforce for a full-time MBA program, gearing up to study for the Graduate Management Admissions Test (GMAT), and drafting a list of potential schools. I completed the ten-month program with Forté in 2015, submitted eight applications, and secured both application fee and GMAT waivers for most applications.

All of the business schools had a variation of an essay prompt that asked for your immediate and long-term goals. I started each of these essays with the exact same three sentences:

My next major professional objective is to return to the private sector as the chief operating officer of a mid-size enterprise within five years. Over the past thirteen years, I have cultivated the skills necessary to oversee customer service, finance, human resources, marketing, performance management, strategy, and technology across a one-hundred-dred-million-dollar-plus organization. I am ready for the next level in my career.

In January 2016, I had my final interview with Stephen Sacca, the then-program director for my top choice, MIT Sloan School of Management's (MIT Sloan) Sloan Fellows MBA Program, by phone as he packed for an overseas trip. I remember him saying, "Asha, you don't need the program; you already have the skills [of an MBA]." To which I replied, "Yes, Stephen, I know that I have the skills, but I need those three letters after my name for credibility." He understood what I meant, and I was accepted into the program within a week and awarded a partial Forté Fellow scholarship by the school.

MIT Sloan secured the top spot on my school selection list because of the school's reputation (ranked fifth on the *US News and World Report* that year and each year since then). The Sloan Fellows MBA is a twelve-month residential program targeted to mid-career executives (my peers) and the school offered hands on action learning labs with global companies. The only drawback of this particular program was it did not provide any career services to its students. The pros outweighed this major con on my list, so I left Ashoka and Washington, DC, to move to Cambridge, MA, in May 2016, becoming a student again after fourteen years.

My decision to immerse myself in academics again proved to be the best decision of my life. Similar to my undergraduate experience, I created a full schedule of academics, student life, and entrepreneurship. The glaring difference was the absence of internships or work to take away from the student experience; this is a deliberate design of MBA programs and I welcomed it. Our core classes and seminars focused on global perspectives, innovation, and leadership. Both my student life and entrepreneurship activities delved into my interests in education and infrastructure. I found ways to work on class projects or events with 70 percent of my classmates in our year together. Most importantly, I found school/life balance, preparing most meals at home, exercising regularly, and sleeping eight hours each night.

Following graduation, I relocated to Buenos Aires, Argentina to continue on my entrepreneurial journey to better understand the Latin American market. I challenged myself in a new country with a new language. I spent eight months understanding the economy, creating a new network of personal and professional contacts, and learning the local ways. I returned to New York in March 2018 with a newfound appreciation for South America and beginning a new job hunt.

NOT REINVENTING THE WHEEL

It had been five years since I completed a job search and participated in job interviews, so I decided to secure some interviews through online job applications before I reached out to my contacts about opportunities in their networks. I hedged that the latter outreach would move fast, so I wanted to be prepared. This time, I kept a spreadsheet of my activity. In six months, I applied to 366 jobs, with an interview selection rate of 7 percent. I believed my qualifications met or exceeded the requirements listed in the job descriptions. When I received rejections for 44 percent of those jobs within twenty-four to forty-eight hours of applying, I came to realize an internal candidate may already be selected for the role or another candidate was further along in the process. I figured that out by monitoring the roles at those organizations on

LinkedIn to see who filled it and their trajectory into that firm. Personally, it became a game to see which job applications would result in an interview.

I also leveraged executive career services offered by both MIT Sloan and GW School of Business (GWSB) as I did in my job search in 2013. At the time, both of my alma maters offered a limited set of complementary hours for alumni to work with a career transition consultant from Right Management. Sandra Buteau became a helpful sounding board during the job search journey. When the three hours ran out with the first school's offering, I was able to continue them with the second school's offering of five hours, without having to change consultants. Through a combination of efficient fifteen-minute check-ins and emails, I benefitted from Buteau's guidance for several months.

For my resume, I approached Deb Welke, another career consultant I met during my job search process in 2013 through the GWSB's career services program for students and alumni. I worked with her to refresh my biography, resume, and LinkedIn profile for the executive roles I actively pursued in 2018. Again, the initial spring 2013 interaction with Welke was covered by the complimentary hours provided by GWSB. While the second outreach was my choice, I was in a position where I could afford to pay for her services.

After I updated my resume and secured several interviews, I exported and reviewed my more than two thousand LinkedIn connections to narrow them down to eighteen contacts to understand their companies better. I received responses from 72 percent of them, including Kundra, who, as I shared earlier, offered me a chance to work with him at Sprinklr, a unified customer experience management technology company in New York City. As you can see, my personal outreach had a much higher success rate of conversations than the online job applications. This is why you should laser focus your efforts on cultivating your networks, understanding your skills, and knowing what you want to do.

My operational portfolio at Sprinklr varied across the years, but always contained high-impact, high-visibility projects aligned to corporate values of employee happiness, customer happiness, and growth. I leveraged my transferable skills in a completely new context of a software company, with its own terminology, metrics, and pace. A few days before this book publishes in August 2021, I will celebrate three years at Sprinklr as a vice president of operations.

Six months into the COVID-19 (Coronavirus Disease 2019) pandemic in fall 2020, I joined the Creator Institute to write this book. I saw many qualified professionals embarking on sudden job hunts. Students graduating into the best economic market found themselves with retracted job offers. Given my understanding of how the job hunt could be a lonely process, compounded by social distancing measures, I wanted to use my prior learnings to help. I learned to balance conducting interviews, writing a book manuscript, and marketing the effort, with ruthless prioritization. Honestly, it helped me to create necessary time boundaries on my shift to remote working.

My aspiration to become a COO of a privately-held technology company continues as I enter the third decade of my career. For me, the role is the ultimate way to bring together the best practices of my insights from different functional roles to propel a company forward.

REFLECTION

I explored a variety of work environments, gained tremendous experience, and built a professional network in multiple cities. I never became an investment banker, but I have an exciting career. A quick glance at my resume or LinkedIn may not make sense at first, but now, you know that referrals appreciated my transferable skills and triggered the twists and turns in my career. Some of those paths required time and patience. Most importantly, my career pivots aligned to my career intentions.

Epstein reminded us in *Range*, "As you pursue a range of experiences and develop new skills or take your skills and apply them to new problems, remember this: it's going to feel inefficient and messy, but that's a great sign that you're learning because the most effective form of learning is never smooth or easy."

Another finding from Epstein was to avoid the doubts: "One study shows early career specializers jump out to an earnings lead after college, but that later specializers made up for the head start by finding work that better fit their skills and personalities."

Some of you may be wondering how I was able to keep paying the bills during these transition periods—it took some time, but I learned to save money in an emergency fund, so I could take my time with any future job search and not worry about paying expenses to drive my motivation. Think of it as an investment in your future self!

Others may question how I stayed motivated during those gaps—I kept busy by creating a schedule that made sure that I had an activity every day, limited my shopping expenses, and kept a normal social life, so I did not feel like I missed out. When interview processes took longer than I expected, I stayed patient by trusting the person working within the company to come through (and they did). While some companies are well-oiled machines in the recruiting area, most are not, so it takes time, even if an employee advocates on your behalf.

MY TRANSFERABLE SKILLS

My story and the next thirteen stories highlight amazing career journeys, where each person's transferable skills were recognized by a connection who opened a door to their next professional opportunity. I conclude each of these chapters summarizing the top three transferable skills for each protagonist, so you can start to identify them in yourself. I will also summarize mine here.

My Key Skills:

- Critical thinking, which I harnessed by applying transferable concepts to improve different work environments.

- Fearless networking, which I developed during my 2013 job search as I found executives to be approachable in person and online.
- Focus, which I used to stay aligned with my professional goals.

Infographic Key

	KEY
Academics	▲
Private sector	■
Public sector	◆
Non-Profit sector	●
Advisory role	★

Asha Aravindakshan

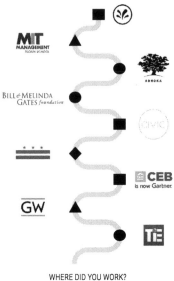

WHERE DID YOU WORK?

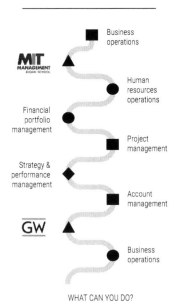

WHAT CAN YOU DO?

STORIES OF CAREER REINVENTION

———

"There are three sorts of people in the world: those who are immovable, people who don't get it, or don't want to do anything about it; those who are movable, people who see the need for change and are prepared to listen to it; and those who move, people who make things happen."

—BENJAMIN FRANKLIN

By wanting to identify your transferable skills, you are movable. When you can pair that understanding with the methods to approach your professional and personal networks, you can move towards career success.

The next section provides you with powerful reference points through career journeys told by real career pivoters. The section is organized by the industry the person worked in during summer 2021: community development, entrepreneurship, marketing, and technology. It is by no means exhaustive, but their career paths are diverse. These career pivoters experienced an average of six career changes, starting their professional lives in fields including accounting, engineering, entertainment, management consulting, and youth engagement. Most are in the second or third decade of their career, so you can see how their transferable skills came through at different points of time. Some also have graduate degrees, so you understand how the decision to pursue higher education advanced or provided a reset button to their career.

Their stories illustrate the ups and downs associated with making dramatic career shifts. As I documented each of their stories for this book, the truth of their life decisions constantly surprised me, especially since their public profiles did not reflect all the details. These characters have depth and their stories have breadth. Five-time Chief Executive Officer (CEO) Margaret Heffernan shared in her 2019 TEDSummit talk, "We have to start thinking about 'just in case,' preparing for events that are generally certain, but specifically, remain ambiguous. Preparedness, coalition-building, imagination, experiments, bravery—in an unpredictable age, these are tremendous sources of resilience and strength... [they] give us limitless capacity for adaptation, variation, and invention... hone and develop them, we can make any future we choose." Heffernan's advice enforces that transferable skills feed resilience, which is a common trait among career pivoters, along with ambition, leadership, and industriousness.

While many set an intention to make a change in their career, there are some who experience hardship and setbacks. This adversity is seen not only in the form of job loss, but also the self-realization of limitations in their capabilities. Those moments of personal growth are difficult when you go through them, but all have value in hindsight. Author

Elizabeth Gilbert faced the difficulty of this insight when she came to terms that her second book would not be as successful as her first (*Eat, Pray, Love*) by acknowledging, "I had to ask myself if I should just quit while I was behind and give up and spare myself this pain. But then, I would find my resolve, and always in the same way, but saying, 'I'm not going to quit, I'm going home.'" For Gilbert, her figurative home was writing and her lifelong love of the work of writing. She found her skills to be a source of strength to move on from failure.

The narratives also provide you with examples you can use to reflect on your own experiences and plot your course ahead. At the end of each chapter, you will find an infographic representation of each career pivoter's story. The image has two components: the first graphic is similar to what you may see on their resume or LinkedIn profile with their companies, but I distinguish the sector of the organization, and the second graphic indicates the main skill they learned in that environment. The illustrations are my interpretation of the portfolio of skills each person accumulated in their career. My decision to choose a curved line was intentional; a straight line did not seem appropriate for their nontraditional career paths. As you read these stories, keep track of your transferable skills, so you can visualize your own career to discover a new narrative.

When you are on the move, it is hard to slow down. Let's see where a pivot can take you!

COMMUNITY
DEVELOPMENT

CHAPTER TWO

LYNSEY FARRELL: FROM YOUTH ADVOCATE TO ANTHROPOLOGY PROFESSOR

A few months after I joined Ashoka, Lynsey Farrell joined the organization to manage a large unwieldy grant. She sat a few offices down the hall from me on the twentieth floor of Ashoka's headquarters. At the same, she was a doctor of philosophy (PhD) candidate preparing her dissertation, so I kept tabs on her progress toward that achievement. Farrell had more energy and know-how than her project required, so I constantly encouraged her to take on more responsibilities, which I learned she did a few years in. Farrell's story is one that zigzagged across the US and Africa over two decades. Let's follow her path to understand the acute aha moments in her career.

Farrell grew up surrounded by the performing arts near Phoenix, Arizona. Her parents founded a community theater called Theater Works, where Farrell spent all her free time throughout her formative years. As a child, she toured with their KidsAlive! youth education program around the US, singing songs about peace during the Cold War in the late eighties and early nineties. She recalled working in the original theater set in a barn in the West Valley, rotating through a variety of roles, including stage manager, box office representative, and workshop facilitator.

Even as Farrell enrolled at Linfield College (now called Linfield University) in Oregon, she continued in a part-time work-study role creating costumes for school productions. Once she took a cultural anthropology class in her sophomore year, the subject matter resonated with her and she found her focus area. She recalled, "All of the questions that I wanted to ask about the world, about life, that were interesting to me, were answered in the types of ways that cultural anthropology engages the world. Everything melded together."

The school's curriculum incorporated an opportunity to study abroad during her junior year, but Farrell's choices were limited because she was not fluent in a language other than English. Her advisor, also an anthropologist, recommended she focus on anglophone (English-speaking) countries in Africa: Ghana, Kenya, and Zimbabwe. Three applications later into arts-themed immersion programs offered by the School for International Training in these three countries, Farrell packed her bags for Harare, Zimbabwe in fall 1999 for the most transformative experience in her life.

During her first week in Harare, Farrell received a cold "go away" from the program director, who instructed each of the students to leave the school and come back in three hours. She did not expect this cultural shock to greet her in a new country, but Farrell managed to figure it out, with friendly locals buying her lunch as she explored the downtown area. This is how she first came head-to-head with the African value of reciprocity, a term from her cultural anthropology classes, defined as an immediate or delayed exchange of goods and services. It set the tone for her experiences.

A few months into her semester abroad, she embarked on a month-long qualitative research project on how cultural children's programming contributed to youth development. This independent study evolved into her senior thesis, of which she said, "I had to figure out what to research, who to interview, where to go. It became the equivalent to the type of research completed by actual anthropologists and I learned that I was good at it."

At one point in the study, she observed a children's theatrical performance in a field outside of Harare. During the event, an organizer nearly twice her age turned to Farrell to ask, "What should we do now? How do we fix our lives here?"

This set of rhetorical questions stumped Farrell: "I was twenty years old. I'd never been here before and I didn't know what to say. From that moment, I had to be a mission-driven socially responsible human being. There was a purpose built into my life."

Farrell returned to Linfield to conclude her junior year of college. In summer 2000, she chose to explore domestic poverty by interning as a park ranger at Canyon de Chelly National

Monument, a national park in Chinle, Arizona, situated on the biggest Navajo reservation in the US. She worked in the visitor center, taking tourists on geology and petroglyph pictograph walks, as well as partnering with Native American guides on campfire talks.

Fueled by these cross-continent experiences, Farrell realized studying anthropology provided her with "an avenue to get to the underlying structures of social interactions." When her social theory class proved to be more intense than she and her classmates expected, Farrell brought together the students for a "social theory study hall," similar to a campfire session where she would facilitate the conversations about the material. This community-building exercise, along with her observations of her professors and advisors, led her to conclude she wanted to be an anthropology professor.

Following graduation, Farrell returned to Africa in early spring 2002, settling in Nairobi, Kenya for a Fulbright research project. As she became situated as an expatriate, locals opened doors to meetings with officials of nongovernmental and governmental entities, specifically in the development sector. After a chance meeting with the executive director of Youth Agenda, a youth advocacy lobbying organization, she carved out an unpaid opportunity with them.

For eighteen months, she attended meetings between Youth Agenda and local officials, using her participant observation techniques from her studies to keep track of the conversations and promised outcomes. She built many relationships with locals and expatriates alike, including Kelly Jo Bahry, who would go from working on the US refugee resettlement program in Kenya as a graduate student to launching the American University (AU) Nairobi program. These interactions also cemented Farrell's choice to help youth in her career.

She recalls this moment in light of the reciprocity she learned in Harare a couple years earlier: "I'm always doing something. I'm always contributing in some way. It was easy for me to not be in the way, to not take away resources. I could give, give, give, knowing later, I can reach back out for help."

Farrell moved to Boston, MA, to start her PhD studies at Boston University (BU), one of the premier African studies programs in the US, in fall 2003. The seeds she planted upon her return from her first trip to Africa now bloomed, as she invested more time in her studies. Each summer, she returned to Kenya, working on development projects through a nongovernmental organization called Carolina for Kibera and fostering the relationships she had been building for the past five years. By summer 2007, Farrell completed her comprehensive exams, which are the second to last hurdle before a dissertation in the PhD process, received approval to write her dissertation prospectus, and secured research funding to return to Kenya full time.

During this same time, Bahry planned her departure from AU Nairobi and reached out to Farrell to see if she had an interest in succeeding her. The role combined Farrell's three passions: youth, development, and Kenya. She remembered their phone call: "Bahry encouraged me to apply, then she told them [AU] to hire me." Following an on-campus visit with the AU Abroad team, Farrell accepted the offer and kept herself busy until the role began in spring 2008.

In the period between her arrival to Nairobi and her start with AU Nairobi, one of Farrell's former colleagues from the Youth Agenda, Joseph Simekha, invited her to join his strategic planning consultancy, Projects and Allied Consulting Limited, as an on-call associate consultant. Farrell assisted Simekha on strategic planning projects in the development sector for three years part time. He taught the aspects of the strategic planning process to her. Once again, her participant observation and interview techniques helped her to build trust with each project's constituents.

Six months after she arrived, the Kenyan national election erupted in violence, greatly impacting the region of Kibera. Carolina for Kibera became a hub for distributing aid. Following the receipt of a sizable donation, Salim Mohamed, the then executive director, reached out to Farrell for help managing the grant. Relying on what she learned from working with Mohamed and the Carolina for Kibera staff for the past four summers, she partnered with a community liaison to set up their peace programming, including mediation trainings, radio spots, and guerrilla theater to meet the requirements outlined in the grant. When I asked how she knew how to manage the grant and programming, Farrell hearkened back to her roots at Theater Works, admitting, "I've never been trained in management, but it's always been natural to me to organize."

Finally, in spring 2008 Farrell and Bahry transitioned responsibilities for AU Nairobi. For four years, Farrell thrived in the role of program director, interacting with twenty-five to thirty mission-driven students each academic year, while completing her dissertation research. She created new programming, such as a week-long home stay for the visiting students with families living in rural areas, and she expanded the range of organizations offering internships by leveraging her extensive local network. In turn, she gave back to these organizations by structuring the internships with talented undergraduate students. These experiences greatly impacted the students, with some of them choosing careers in development and others who discovered it was not for them. Remembering her own experience in Harare, she would tell her students to "figure it out" when they arrived with challenges at her door. One year, the students jokingly rewarded this advice with an honorific "figure it out" statue.

Farrell returned to BU to focus on her dissertation. In early 2013, she met Joanna Davidson, an assistant professor specializing in Africanist anthropology, who served as a reader of her dissertation. Davidson read Farrell's dissertation on youth in Kenya, connected the dots on her capabilities, and recommended she consider a new role at Ashoka. Davidson worked at Ashoka nearly twenty years before and continued to be involved with their fellowship selection process. Davidson passed Farrell's resume onto Bev Schwartz, who ran Ashoka's marketing team and managed a multi-million-dollar grant from the Mastercard Foundation for solutions for youth employment in sub-Saharan Africa. After a five-month interview process, Farrell secured the grant management role and moved to Washington, DC.

Her decision surprised her academic peers who did not understand how she translated her skills. She realized those without work experience did not know how to talk about their forays in program management or leading research teams into a professional career. On PhDPortals.com in January 2021, Dana Vioreanu recommended, "If you get a job or collaboration that is somehow related to your PhD, this situation will be very helpful for your overall learning performance. It will keep you focused on thinking and finding new ideas for your PhD thesis and it will increase the chances of being a top PhD student."

Farrell began to understand the world of systems change, which addresses the root cause of social problems, fostered by Ashoka and its fellowship of social entrepreneurs around the globe. In parallel, she took on the arduous task of rightsizing the grant budget and reporting, building relationships with African organizations, and monitoring the impact of the work. I watched her take on these tasks—it was no small feat. Farrell spent the majority of her five and a half years at Ashoka managing the strict requirements of the Future Forward grant.

Eighteen months into her tenure at Ashoka, Farrell completed her PhD. She remembered a conversation we had in fall 2015, where I advised her, "You could do something else." I could see the grant management work was not fulfilling, and she was in a funny place in the marketing department because of the executive relationships with the donor. A year later, Ashoka embraced Farrell's gifts and she stepped into a newly formed business operations role for the African region. However, she quickly became inundated by the administrative tasks, which languished under prior leadership and felt, "I was trying to do too many jobs at the same time. It was a messy, chaotic period. I tried to clean up a lot of things."

Finally, after two years of bringing discipline to the four regional offices in Africa, repairing their relationships with the headquarters teams, and working on a strategy with new leadership, Farrell stepped out of the business operations role in summer 2018. She joined the global venture fellowship team to produce a first-time report about the social entrepreneurs who were selected to be Ashoka fellows that year. To facilitate this study, she used the evaluation methods from her PhD to develop a qualitative analysis tool to deal with the multitudes of data procured through the extensive fellowship selection process. Farrell published the sixty-page "Emerging Insights: Ashoka Fellows 2018" report and assisted with the 2019 report as a consultant.

In winter 2018, Farrell spotted a unique job opening at the University of Pennsylvania on the H-Africa listserv, which targeted academics interested in Africa. It listed a dual role: senior lecturer in anthropology and director of the Africa program at the Lauder Institute. The responsibilities included teaching an African studies course, running a summer program in Africa, advising legal and MBA students, and being a thought leader. She called it a "half-teacher, half-administrator" role, which seemed to be written for her. She secured the role in spring 2019. When her peers asked her how she returned to academia, she pointed out, "It's because of this one particular job. No other job exists like it."

At the time of our conversation, Farrell planned the annual Africa Symposium for spring 2021, bringing together experts from the US and Africa to a virtual two-day conference on the "Future of Work in 21st-Century Africa." She reached out to professional networks across Africa and within Ashoka to fill the speaker roster. A week before the conference, the tickets sold out. For Farrell, her invitation to speak at the conference was her moment of reciprocity.

Farrell's exploration of a liberal arts curriculum helped her discover the field of anthropology and her advisors became role models as she pursued her PhD. While it took twelve years, she knowingly took the trade off on time to build her career. She highlighted the benefits of working while completing her PhD: "I am really blessed. I was able to support many organizations."

Farrell's Key Skills:

- Active listening, which Farrell learned in her anthropology classes, then put into practice in her field work.
- Compassion, which Farrell carried with her through her experiences, always keeping youth at the forefront of her work and studies.
- Facilitation, which Farrell initially learned in the theater, then applied to discussions in her nonprofit and advisory roles.

Farrell honed her managerial skills in Theater Works and saw them flourish in the nongovernmental organizations she worked with in Kenya and the US. In turn, she adopted the value of reciprocity in her approach of building relationships that have lasted a lifetime. My takeaway from her story is that the perfect role can come along, but you need to keep your eyes open for it.

Lynsey Farrell

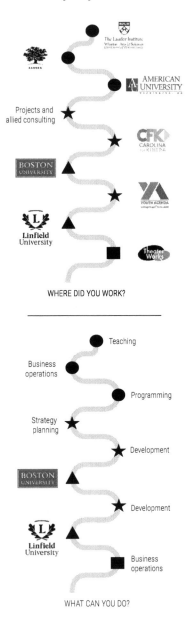

WHERE DID YOU WORK?

Teaching

Business operations

Programming

Strategy planning

Development

Development

Business operations

WHAT CAN YOU DO?

CHAPTER THREE

GRAHAM PLASTER: FROM MILITARY DIPLOMAT TO COMMUNITY MANAGER

———

Graham Plaster is on a mission to help veterans upskill their careers. A mutual friend and his Naval Academy classmate, Josh Welle, connected us. However, my conversation with Plaster uncovered a veteran with many career pivots of his own. Plaster's story starts at a crossroad.

Plaster studied English and wanted to teach at the Naval Academy, but the past five years he spent on a ship deepening his leadership skills were not part of a traditional path to the prerequisite doctorate degree. Instead, during the 2009 recession in the US, he pursued higher education in the form of a master's in humanities from Salve Regina University in Newport, RI. As he met nearby US Naval War College professors with specialties in the Middle East and explored curriculum at Brown University, where "they were doing a lot of stuff with digital media under the umbrella of comparative literature," he focused his own comparative literature coursework on social media in Iran.

This peculiar choice had been shaped by Plaster's under-standing of the geopolitical issues surrounding the June 2009 Green Movement in Iran. Jared Keller described this historical movement in *The Atlantic*, stating, "Western media outlets were filled with a flurry of reports of protesters using Twitter, e-mail, blogs, and text messages to coordinate rallies, share information, and locate compatriots. Journalists were agape at the sudden influx of information coming out of the country, unusual in light of the Iranian authorities' media blackout."

Plaster's choice to study humanities with a focus on social media trends was timely as he saw organic digital groups sprouting up on Facebook, LinkedIn, and Twitter, eclipsing institutional networks. He shared a case study about National Public Radio (NPR) with me, commenting, "After a couple of years of seeing how successful Facebook was at bringing people together, NPR decides it's time to set up their own community. They find an existing, unofficial group of NPR fans run by a volunteer that is already very large, and they realize that they may never see that many fans join their own community. So, they approach the volunteer to turn his unofficial community into an official one... it made his day! Now, that was a beautiful picture of what can happen between organic networks and institutions."

Following the completion of his master's degree in 2009, Plaster applied to be a US Navy foreign area officer, part of their diplomatic community, and joined their language training program at the Defense Language Institute Foreign Language Center in Monterrey, CA. His intention to study Farsi, or Persian, to deepen his knowledge of Iran, was greeted with, "That's great that you're interested in Iran, but we don't really need any Farsi speakers right now. We need a bunch of Arabic speakers, given the current focus on Iraq." Plaster found the language program to be challenging, admitting, "I don't have a natural ability with languages. I really struggled with Arabic, and they placed me in an accelerated course. It wasn't a great start on the path towards being a linguist."

Once he finished the training, Plaster moved to Washington, DC, in 2010 taking on work in the Pentagon supporting the United Nations peacekeeping operations. He joined several professional networking groups, including the Foreign Area Officer Association, and through a chain of introductions, ended up advising some intelligence community officials on emerging technology, social networks, and Middle Eastern politics. When he completed his active duty in 2013, Plaster became a lieutenant commander in the US Navy Reserves and began a six-year consulting stint as a senior policy advisor at the Pentagon. He reflected, "It was kind of a pseudo-anthropologist role, where my master's degree qualified me for that. It was a pivot towards policy. It was a great job because it was broad—it allowed me to use my humanities-type background and military-type background to interface with lots of different types of people."

Most importantly, he became a volunteer administrator for a LinkedIn group called "The Intelligence Community," which had thirteen thousand national security professionals as members. Plaster leveraged the group to launch a company around the premise of providing a social network for national security professionals. Now, he could apply what he learned about social networks to his own, which resulted in its expansion to 120,000 members in less than ten years.

Plaster channeled his energy into writing two books, *In the Shadow of Greatness: Voices of Leadership, Sacrifice, and Service of the Naval Academy Class of 2002*, coauthored by Welle and their classmates from the Naval Academy, and *Hacking the Job Search: How to Escape the Rat Race of Unread Résumés and Unanswered Applications*. The latter designed to help those leaving military services to search for a job using social media and social networks, but in a sensitive way, given the confidential nature of their jobs. He also served as the editor in chief of *Foreign Area Officer Association Journal of International Affairs* for several years.

In spring 2019, Plaster met an executive from TDX Corporation, a conglomerate based out of Alaska, through Intelligence Community Inc. about a potential job opportunity. After a few conversations, TDX created a vice president role for Plaster, with responsibilities in sales and business development. This foray into the private sector was lucrative, as Plaster remarks, "It had a higher upside. It's always exciting as an entrepreneur or as someone in business development to say, 'Today, I'm going to get up and I'm going to earn more.' It felt like a better fit than the policy work that I've been in." Plaster found success in the role by reaching out to his professional networks about business opportunities with TDX. He believed "the next generation of business development will be done by the social networking ninjas who really know how to leverage LinkedIn, because LinkedIn has the network effect of people who are commercially interested."

While Plaster did not earn a doctorate, he certainly spent many hours honing his skills to teach others how to use social networks for diplomacy, career transitions, and business development. Plaster's ability to combine his cutting-edge studies on social networks and day-to-day work with intelligence professionals into his Intelligence Community Inc. is a neat blend of personal and professional interests. The synergy of the Intelligence Community, Inc. network created by Plaster and the member's professional pursuits led him to mentor hundreds of startup founders in the national security sector.

Claire Madden is a social researcher that delivered a 2015 TEDx Talk, where she said, "Traditional leadership styles have been based on linearity and conformity, based on position and hierarchy. However, the leadership styles that the younger generations are responding more to are those based on collaboration and communication, where they can participate and have a voice." Plaster's forward-thinking approach to Intelligence Community Inc. cultivated a multigenerational, peer-to-peer community of veterans, where they can learn from each other.

Plaster's Key Skills:

- Mentorship, which Plaster developed in his continuous work supporting veterans in their career transitions to civilian life and entrepreneurship.
- Understanding of social media, which Plaster formally studied, then cultivated through the Intelligence Community Inc. virtual community.

- Writing, which Plaster invested in his two books, industry publication, and personal blog.

While Plaster could apply his key skills at the Pentagon, he could also leverage them outside of work in his passion projects. He showed how he did not need to pursue further education to cultivate his skills; instead, he pursued entrepreneurial endeavors that were as challenging, if not more. We can learn from Plaster's example that we can forge our own paths using our skills.

Graham Plaster

WHERE DID YOU WORK?

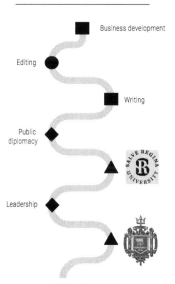

WHAT CAN YOU DO?

CHAPTER FOUR

JENNIFER LEIGHTON-GUZMAN: FROM FUNDRAISER TO CHECK WRITER

———

Jennifer Leighton-Guzman and I both joined the board of directors of the GW Alumni Association in 2013, with similar intentions to engage the alumni community, but our paths to the university and the alumni association were vastly different.

Leighton-Guzman always knew she wanted to go to college, despite not having role models with college degrees. When she was six years old, her late mother took her to visit the University of Houston Hines College of Architecture campus. The trip left an impression on a young Leighton-Guzman as she recalled, "I still remember seeing students in the classroom." Their modest outings also included local visits to wealthy neighborhoods, where her mother would reiterate the message, "If you want to live in a house like this one day, you have to go to college. You have to work hard; you have to pave your own path." Her middle school years included a period where they were homeless, rotating through her aunt's house and motels from week to week.

The September 11th tragedy impacted Leighton-Guzman greatly. She felt shocked that anyone would want to hurt the country in such a cruel way. A few months later in January 2002, her high school organized a senior class trip to Washington, DC, through Close Up DC, a one-week immersion program to the nation's capital with visits to Capitol Hill, monuments, and embassies. Leighton-Guzman fell in love with the nation's capital and knew she wanted to study political science there.

While her mom could not afford the tuition for a private university, Leighton-Guzman felt undeterred. She worked two full-time jobs and completed a Congressional internship, while attending Lone Star College-North Harris Community College. She saved enough money to complete one college application, applied as a transfer student to The George Washington University, and was accepted into to the class of 2006. According to the National Association for College Admission Counseling's 2016 Admission Trends Survey, the average admit rate for transfer applicants is 62 percent, with 54 percent of the transfer students coming from a community college. She beat the odds. Leighton-Guzman's outlook shifted: "I got the acceptance letter. It was like my life literally changed. I knew that a door had been opened and I needed to be responsible for that opportunity."

Following her graduation from GW, Leighton-Guzman moved to San Antonio in search of a full-time job. She attended a job fair in spring 2007, where she struck up a conversation with Belinda Benavidez in the line to enter the hall. Benavidez graduated with a political science degree a few years earlier. Upon hearing Leighton-Guzman was a recent college graduate not employed yet, Benavidez gave her life-changing advice: "Instead of applying to a job full time, have you thought about volunteering full time?"

Armed with this advice, which Leighton-Guzman repeats to other young people to this day, she switched her job search strategy to secure two part-time volunteer roles, working twenty hours each with the Alzheimer's Association, where Benavidez worked, and the Girl Scouts of Southwest Texas. A few months in, the Girl Scouts offered a full-time role to Leighton-Guzman. Her big bet had paid off.

Leighton-Guzman stepped into a newly created role of teen program manager with the Girl Scouts in fall 2007. The program's coverage expanded from eight to twenty-one counties in Texas, which impacted nearly a quarter of the state's population. While Leighton-Guzman did not have the requisite management experience for the position, she felt the hiring managers overlooked it, explaining, "I could connect with the teenage girls because I was close in age to them." She took the responsibility with gusto, managing the existing leadership programs and starting new ones, like a robotics program.

She quickly learned that in a nonprofit, "you wear twenty-five hats. These programs were expensive to run, so I needed to learn how to fundraise." Emilio Hinojosa, a grant writer who became her mentor, brought her to meetings with donors where she could observe how he asked for money for the Girl Scouts programming. Together, they worked on grant applications, to secure funding for the teen program offerings, which also improved her writing. At the same time, Leighton-Guzman started a part-time master's in public administration at the University of Texas in San Antonio, completing the degree during her three-year tenure with the Girl Scouts.

When she started her career and graduate school, Leighton-Guzman did not have a professional network in San Antonio to lean on. She reached out to GW to join the local alumni chapter, but there was none. However, the school, seeing her interest and enthusiasm, connected her with Jim Eskin, an alumni and San Antonio resident of twenty-five years. Both worked in development, another commonality, and together, they launched the San Antonio alumni chapter for GW in 2007. After a few years of working together to host events engaging students and alumni, she shared her intentions to find a new role. He put forth an opening for a development coordinator with the Texans Can Academy in San Antonio. Eskin was part of a volunteer fundraising board for the charter school, which advised the school's leadership to create a full-time role to take on the development work. He pointed out, "I can teach you how to fundraise and grant write, but I can't you teach how to connect with the community or kids." Her natural ability to build relationships stood out to him during their time forming the GW San Antonio alumni chapter.

Leighton-Guzman was a shoo-in for the role with Eskin's support. From fall 2010, she spent the year building the development function for the charter school and participating in school activities, including becoming the assistant basketball coach for the girls' team. When her and Matt, her future husband, relocated from San Antonio to Houston, Leighton-Guzman continued her role as a development director with the Texans Can Academy in Houston.

Two years into the Houston-based role and six years into her career, Leighton-Guzman took her professional expertise working with youth to heart: "These experiences made me realize that there's so much that needs to be done in the community and there's so much throwing of checks around by corporations, but the corporations don't even know the struggles of those in the community. How can you support the community or build a plan to support the community, if you don't even know the struggles of the community or you've never been around somebody who is struggling?"

She sought a new position, recounting, "I wanted something that would leverage my experience, my studies, and my desire to do something a bit more meaningful in the world." She phoned Richard Mauldin, her Dallas-based liaison for the Texas Capital Bank (TCB), which was a donor to the Texans Can Academy, and she spoke candidly about any opportunities on his team: "I love your job. If there's ever an opportunity to join your team, I would love to work for you." Two weeks later, he returned her call. The bank carved out his responsibilities for the Houston area in a brand-new role.

Leighton-Guzman earnestly joined TCB as its first community development officer in spring 2013, taking on an enormous responsibility. She started off by doing what she does best—building relationships with people in similar positions at other banks, asking them informational interview questions such as, "What are you doing? How did you start this program? What did you focus on?" She learned that, because of the regulatory nature of financial services, each bank produced its own unique plan for community engagement. She had to get up to speed on the specifics of the Community Reinvestment Act (CRA), which, while enacted in 1977, had subsequent updates to its regulations.

While the bank's executives had to make sure its investing, lending, giving, and serving were equitable according to the CRA guidelines, Leighton-Guzman's day-to-day activities focused on the "how you do it" for society. She relied upon the community relationships she crafted in the previous two years to find partners for her programming efforts. As the bank grew from nine billion dollars to thirty-eight billion dollars' worth of assets under management, TCB hired additional community development officers in other major cities and replicated the programs Leighton-Guzman incubated for Houston statewide.

One of the most important duties of a bank is responding to community needs in times of natural disasters, such as hurricanes or floods, both of which plague Houston. Banks provide lending to support disaster recovery efforts or give to organizations to help people in need. Leighton-Guzman summarized it as, "When you are in a position of power, where you can make decisions about where money is funneled and how decisions are made, it's really important to use that responsibly and for the greater good." For example, after Hurricane Harvey hit Houston in August 2017,

Leighton-Guzman's team organized volunteer events for the bank's employees to give back to the community.

In March 2020, at the start of the coronavirus pandemic, TCB repurposed their financial literacy bus into a respite center for hospital employees working at a COVID-19 testing site. They also needed to proactively engage their nonprofit constituents in virtual calls to make sure her team understood, "What are your needs? What were your challenges throughout the year? How can we help or connect you to resources?"

More recently, Houston was devastated by an unprecedented winter storm in February 2021, which caused power outages and water line breaks affecting commercial and residential properties. Leighton-Guzman's team mobilized their efforts to include funding-related requests to repair broken pipes of a nonprofit providing essential services.

Leighton-Guzman always remembers her roots in her native Houston as she finds ways to advance the bank's outreach. She described the community development role as, "I feel like you need to know the struggle. If you have never struggled in your life and have gone without a phone or lights or water or maybe you were homeless, how are you going to know how to connect with that population and know what they need?" She is now a vice president in her eighth year with TCB, a role model serving the Houston community.

Leighton-Guzman worked hard to give herself a better life. She relied on her geniality to open doors, while her programming impact spoke volumes in the community. She lives by the mantra, "Never ever, ever close my eyes to a new opportunity to grow or to do more for the world."

Leighton-Guzman's Key Skills:

- Empathy, which Leighton-Guzman put forward in every situation as she recognized the struggles of other people in her path.
- Fellowship, which Leighton-Guzman built as she created youth communities and an alumni chapter.
- Speaking up, which Leighton-Guzman used to find mentors and new jobs.

From her early days, Leighton-Guzman set far-reaching goals for herself and achieved them, even if she did not have the means initially. She leveraged the relationships that she fostered into mentorship that enabled her to progress in her career. I found her to be cool, calm, and collected in sometimes tense board meetings, which is a gift to mitigate the many stressful situations that may surface in a community seeking assistance from corporations.

Jennifer Leighton-Guzman

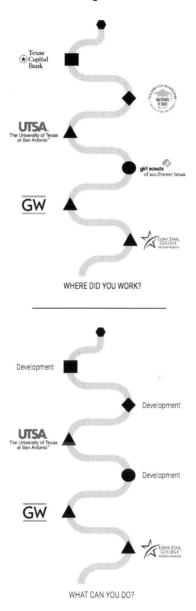

Texas Capital Bank

TEXAS CAN ACADEMIES

UTSA
The University of Texas at San Antonio™

girl scouts
of southwest texas

GW

LONE STAR COLLEGE
NORTH HARRIS

WHERE DID YOU WORK?

Development

Development

UTSA
The University of Texas at San Antonio™

Development

GW

LONE STAR COLLEGE
NORTH HARRIS

WHAT CAN YOU DO?

ENTREPRENEURSHIP

CHAPTER FIVE

ANJALI NAIK: FROM MUSIC ENTREPRENEUR TO ROBOTICS ENTREPRENEUR

———

I can still remember the Monday in May 2002 when Anjali Naik walked into my office in the Watergate office building. Having driven up from Chapel Hill, NC, to Washington, DC, on the day after her college graduation, she sought to immerse herself in the nascent entrepreneurship scene described by local alumni. We became good friends after surviving a turbulent year in TiE DC. While we stayed in touch since then, it was not until our most recent conversation that I understood how she found a home in scaling technology companies.

Naik's story begins in the furniture showroom floors of Salem Furniture Gallery, run by her entrepreneurial father. She watched as he grew the business, both in the size of his vendor partners and customers, as well as the range of offerings. She recalls, "The main thing that I learned from watching my dad was selling. It's how you engage with someone, position the products, and empathize with the customer that encourages them to buy from you versus someone else." During these years, Naik also enjoyed listening to Bollywood music and watching Bollywood movies, which her family rented from a neighboring town forty-five minutes away.

Fast forward to 2002, Naik became a fixture at TiE DC's networking events, interacting with local C-level executives, understanding their expectations to meet cofounders with complementary skill sets or potential investors, and expanding the TiE DC membership to ensure these interactions occurred at our events. She solidified her professional networking skills in a short time. But her heart was not set on the membership-development work.

Naik wanted to work in the media and entertainment industry, so by the end of the year, she packed up her car again to drive out to Los Angeles, CA. She applied for a royalty analyst job at MGM Studios and started in February 2004. Within the first month of her first corporate role, she reported, "It was horrible. I was a cog in a wheel. I was one of twenty analysts in cubicles calculating how much an actor is getting paid for their movie."

One of the newer factors of these movie royalty license agreements was revenue generated from films placed on fledgling video-on-demand services. Naik conducted online research to find out how to secure films, like Bollywood movies, and put them on demand. This research led to her discovering a media startup called 212[MEDIA] that acquired the rights to five Bollywood movies and put them on Time Warner Cable. She emailed the generic mailbox listed on 212[MEDIA]'s website, only to have it bounce back. Undaunted, Naik looked up the company's leadership on the now-defunct social network called Friendster, with success.

After a few months of back-and-forth messaging on her findings about the video-on-demand market and her lifelong passion for Bollywood entertainment, one of the 212[MEDIA] partners, Vinodh Bhat, invited Naik to join them. She agreed to a cofounder role and moved to New York City in April 2005 to focus on the startup's business operations and distribution partnerships. Naik focused on securing the movies on videotapes, then walking them over with self-produced marketing collateral to Time Warner Cable.

As the team grappled with generating steady revenue, their research found music streaming outpaced video-on-demand in the consumer market, which convinced the leadership team to shift its model. Naik also led the effort to rebrand and update the name to Saavn. With these major changes, she managed global partnerships with seventy distribution networks for a music catalog that represented over 80 percent of all Bollywood music. Saavn's revenues increased by multiples because of the shift from movie to music streaming. At Saavn, she found parallels between engaging with people and managing physical goods to online goods, explaining, "We had a similar partnership ecosystem at Salem Furniture Gallery. It doesn't matter what business it is; you're building relationships that help you optimize and scale a business."

Naik moved to San Francisco, CA to join her future husband, Samir, in 2011. Shortly afterward, a friend introduced her to Charlene Soelter at Ten23 Creative for consulting work that turned into full-time employment. Soelter was a creative person who had a knack for selling and constructing elaborate trade show exhibitions for Silicon Valley's biggest technology firms, but she could not manage the business aspect. Naik's project management skills, honed at Saavn, were a complementary fit. She gained exposure to physical design and design-thinking concepts used by the team. She observed how Soelter's kind manners nurtured her customer relationships to grow sales. This approach left an impression on Naik.

As Naik settled into San Francisco, she met a friend that referred her to a new unit at Google called Google Shopping Express. The same-day delivery service started as a pilot in Mountain View, CA, with aggressive plans to expand to seven more cities and needed to multiply its team to make it happen. Naik's interviewer, Ryan Quinlan, appreciated her nontraditional background and brought her on board. I questioned her decision to join a large company after her poor experience at MGM Studios, to which she explained, "When I moved to the Bay Area, I started to wonder what Google was all about. If you're on the outside, you want to know, 'What do they do in there; why does everyone talk about it?'" Now, she would find out.

Naik joined the Shopping Express team in September 2013, quickly discovering that while her previous companies ran lean operations, Google was the opposite. She recalled, "When you have nearly unlimited resources, like at Google, you can see how fast you can scale the business. You're not necessarily doing it in the most efficient way, but at least, you can see the pace of scale, given the number of resources." As they launched in seven new cities, she realized Google was a data-driven organization by nature, with this data typically in aggregate from online users. The product teams were not used to incorporating feedback from an individual in the field into a product's design.

Naik set up a product operations group that quickly consolidated and relayed process improvement feedback from the three hundred field staff to the three-person product team for Shopping Express. She also encouraged the engineers to take "field trips" to work alongside the field staff in the grocery stores to understand their troubles in finding items firsthand, to which they begrudgingly agreed. It opened their eyes to the problems in order fulfillment. Finally, she issued online surveys to capture real-time feedback from the field staff that would eventually end up as features in the product roadmap. Naik experienced a startup lifestyle in a large company as she "set up the structure around an issue, staffed it, then moved onto the next project every two to three months." According to Forrester, you need playbooks based on best practices to minimize risk and accelerate success. Her corporate experience at Google was wildly different from her MGM Studios tenure.

When Naik looked for her next role in 2015, a Googler introduced her to Amit Sharma, the CEO of Narvar, a supply chain technology that enabled a retailer's post-purchase consumer experience. She joined the young team and gained a solid understanding of the product, enough to explain it in sales calls and support customers through their post-sales implementation process. Naik captured technical requests from the customers and wrote them up for the product team, then took a page from Soelter's relationship management playbook. "The big thing that I learned from Charlene was setting up one-on-one weekly calls with as many customers that will take them. If they don't want to meet weekly, then meet biweekly or monthly. Any kind of recurring interaction set up at the beginning helps to cultivate the relationship."

By spring 2017, Naik wanted a change of pace in a part-time role. Sharma introduced her to his former manager, now the CEO of Kindred, which creates autonomous robotics for retailers' warehouses. Her first assignment was to secure their trade show participation and design a booth, a throwback to Naik's Ten23 Creative days. Soon after, she assumed a full-time role focused on how to implement their ten-foot by ten-foot robots in The Gap's warehouse. Her project management prowess emerged as she navigated through multiple hurdles at The Gap. "There were people from different teams involved, creating many approval steps, so I had to keep things moving by setting up weekly calls with them to discuss our deliverables and keep track of the customer-side tasks."

Once a project finished, she continued to nurture the relationship by sharing the project's performance data routinely to show success. She created a repeatable process others could follow, scaling it for every subsequent customer or warehouse that signed up with the company.

Currently, Naik is a cofounder and chief operations officer of Cartken, an autonomous robot for sidewalk deliveries, from her home in Charlotte, NC. In the first year, her responsibilities included pitching to investors, building a go-to-market strategy, and implementing Cartken's robot solution at various customer sites. She shared candidly, "All of these experiences and successes along the way made me feel confident to be a founder again and take on a C-level role at Cartken." It weaved together her experiences seamlessly, not only in furthering the development of the company's core technology, but also with a familiar founding team from Google Shopping Express, including Quinlan, as well as her own reliable playbook of scaling emerging technologies for customer adoption.

Naik's pivots within industry, roles, and cities were frequent, resolute and gutsy. While her surroundings were unfamiliar, the steps to success became solidified with each turn.

Naik's Key Skills:

- Adapting to change, which Naik demonstrated by diving into each of her new surroundings.
- Business analysis, which Naik leveraged to bridge the gaps between the customer experience and product in multiple technology companies.
- Customer first, which Naik strengthened after her Ten23 experience showed her the value of building stakeholder relationships.

Naik learned from the environments around her, like a sponge. She moved from Chapel Hill, NC, to Washington, DC, to Los Angeles, CA, to New York City, NY, to San Francisco, CA, to Charlotte, NC, in pursuit of roles that interested her, shifting from a nonprofit to private sector in a mix of privately-held and publicly-traded companies. She switched between founder and team member, but always stayed true to her operational savvy. It can be daunting to make major shifts, but Naik's story shows you should not constrain your ambition.

Anjali Naik

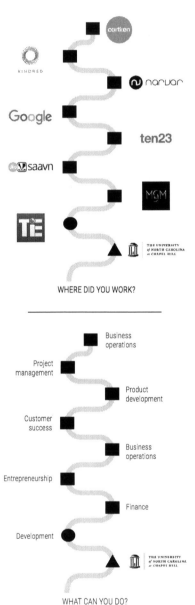

WHERE DID YOU WORK?

WHAT CAN YOU DO?

CHAPTER SIX

JUSTIN NASSIRI: FROM NAVAL OFFICER TO CONTENT STRATEGIST

———

Justin Nassiri hosts a popular podcast devoted to helping veterans with career pivots. I knew he would offer fantastic insights on using transferable skills developed in one job to change your career path. When I interviewed Nassiri, he revealed a veteran with an entrepreneurial streak.

"Once I left the military, there were thousands of options, so I met with older students and alumni to understand my choices," began Nassiri as he described how he crafted his post-military career based on the paths set by his fellow alumni of the Naval Academy. He would complete his service, earn his MBA degree, then launch a career as a management consultant. As far as his decision to complete an MBA, Nassiri viewed himself as a manager and told me, "I enjoyed managing people in the military and thought, well, what's the closest equivalent? It's leading in business, so go to business school. I wrote my business school essays about that, then I told everyone in business school that was my story."

Nassiri immersed himself in student life at the Stanford Graduate School of Business, securing leadership roles among his peers in student clubs. He also met as many other students as he could, "I had coffee with a classmate, who worked previously in investment banking. Literally, I thought he was a teller at a bank. I never heard of this industry, so these chats were a very eye-opening experience."

In Nassiri's interviews for a summer internship with a management consulting firm, he shared a story from his time onboard a submarine: "We used a process to track failed equipment that wasn't working well, so I interviewed everyone on the boat to come up with a different system. In retrospect, it was a creative process—all about finding a solution to a pain point." This problem-solving technique landed him an internship at the prestigious McKinsey & Co. Then, while the world reeled from the stock market crash of March 2009, Nassiri received a full-time job offer from McKinsey with a start date for the February after his graduation. Nassiri marked off the boxes on his career checklist by completing his MBA and securing a full-time role as a management consultant.

Now, for the first time in his life, Nassiri had free time on his hands. As the countdown clock ticked down the seven months until he started at McKinsey, Nassiri toyed around with creating and running a startup based on an idea formulated during his MBA program. He recalls a discussion with a friend: "I was thinking between starting a company or joining a startup for fun. My friend was like, 'Look, if you spend ten thousand dollars in six months starting a company and it doesn't work out, then at least, you get a story to tell a friend over a beer one day. It's worth it.'" Of course, Nassiri had a failsafe: if the startup did not work out in the allotted time or he ran out of the initial investment, then he could continue with his plan to become a management consultant the following year.

Nassiri launched StoryBox, a marketing technology startup, in summer 2009 and raised venture capital funding two weeks later. He loved what he did as an entrepreneur. He found an outlet for his creativity in his daily work, mentioning, "The creative returns for me were high enough, enjoyable enough." The primary interviews he enjoyed conducting on the ship now manifested as user research interviews for product design. So, he reneged on the full-time job offer from McKinsey, much to the chagrin of both Stanford and his parents, even paying back a signing bonus large enough to buy a car.

As Nassiri built out StoryBox, he utilized his professional networks to search and hire a technical cofounder and team members. He hired people he thought could be fine working with ambiguity or uncertainty, as he did. He quickly learned he did not thrive on managing people, as he convinced himself for the past decade. Four years into the experience, he did not enjoy the management aspect of the CEO role—the managing the team, conducting difficult conversations with employees, or pushing them to squeeze out an extra 10 percent in each workday. He reflected, "Managing was the most draining activity for me. The lesson for me was radical self-honesty, self-knowledge, and a willingness to lean into what is both most enjoyable and what I'm best at." Instead, under the guidance of an executive coach, he clearly saw that "[his] skill set is being able to bring a new idea to life quickly, with very little resources and to operate with an extreme amount of ambiguity." In time, his parents came to recognize their son loved his creative work as Justin reflected, "My passion came through over the phone, even when I was working on a Friday at nine o'clock at night. They understood I am enjoying what I am doing."

Seven years into his tenure at StoryBox, Nassiri launched the *Beyond the Uniform* podcast for military career transition advice. Within three years, he produced 385 corporate-sponsored podcasts, featuring US Navy Sea, Air, and Land Teams (SEALS), Army Rangers, and National Football League players, that reached 250,000 streams across seventy-eight countries. Nassiri structured a team of consultants to edit the content in a formulaic way, so he did not have to rely on a single employee to handle the work and could scale it accordingly. Through his podcasts, he found, "The best gift that I can give people is the concept of iteration. People put so much pressure on themselves to find a job that they're going to do for the next ten years, rather than 'what's the lily pad where I can build a skill set, get a taste of whether I want to do this.'" Iteration means you repeat and adjust your actions to get closer to your end goal. Nassiri learned to iterate between his two professional experiences, and he extracted that similar narrative from those he interviewed.

From what Nassiri saw in the exponential growth of the podcast industry, he launched his second venture, Captivate, which helps businesses convert long-form content (such as podcasts or webinars) into multiple smaller clips for social media consumption. Leveraging the model he built for

Beyond the Uniform, he put together a team of consultants for the day-to-day work that allowed him to manage the creative part instead. Initially, he set up distinct teams that produced blogs and videos. After he saw a pattern emerge, he admitted, "When I first started, I thought that blog posts would be a really big piece, but it's turned out that video has been the lion's share. One of the advantages of building in the way that I am building is nothing is sacred. If blog posts are irrelevant, it's out of what we do. I can adjust the resources quickly."

Nassiri's voice became upbeat as he described the new structure, stating, "I focused on hiring a lot of contractors and documenting processes. I focus on discrete measures of performance. If someone's not working out, I can give the procedure to someone else. Everything's easier for me from a contracting lens." With this arrangement, he already decided that when he secures investment in Captivate, he will be upfront with future investors about his decision to not continue as CEO, advise they hire someone good at managing people, and concentrate on the creative aspects of the firm.

Noemie Delfassy explained in her 2016 TEDxLSE Talk, "Our all-powerful mind thinks it knows better, and it blinds us from seeing reality as it is, and we become stubborn in our ways. I call that a blind spot." In scientific terms, a blind spot is a cognitive bias, which are systematic errors in thinking that lead us to deviate from a standard of rationality or good judgement. Delfassy, an MBA turned entrepreneur like Nassiri, advised, "Whatever your bias is, be aware that you probably should be doing a lot of other things that you're not as comfortable doing; go do them quickly. Be aware in identifying certain biases that you may have. Face the hard truths; don't hide from them. Accept imperfections."

Nassiri explored a handful of options since leaving the military, but his ability to iterate on his own career stood out to me. He quoted *So Good They Can't Ignore You* by Cal Newport, saying, "What builds satisfaction is expertise, but make sure you find something that you want to be an expert at. Had I built my life to identify around management, I might not have been willing to let that go and go in this different direction."

Nassiri's Key Skills:

- Creativity, which Nassiri set as the basis of both of his content marketing technology companies.
- Self-awareness, which allowed Nassiri to discover the work environments he would thrive in.
- User research, which Nassiri first developed in his Navy experience, then refined in both ventures and podcast interviews.

Nassiri imagined his career and plotted the steps without knowing the full extent of the skills he enjoys. He could have used volunteer experiences or internship opportunities to discover more about his likes and dislikes, as he now recommends to others: "I'm a big fan of internships or volunteer experiences. You don't need six months; you need two weeks' time to figure out 'is this the size company that I want to work in, is this the industry, is this the functional role I want, maybe I need to be in a smaller company or a bigger company, [and] is this the geographic area.' We put too much pressure on ourselves rather than just iterating, iterating, and iterating." When you find a career that is interesting to you, see if you can volunteer or create an adult internship opportunity to explore the fit.

Justin Nassiri

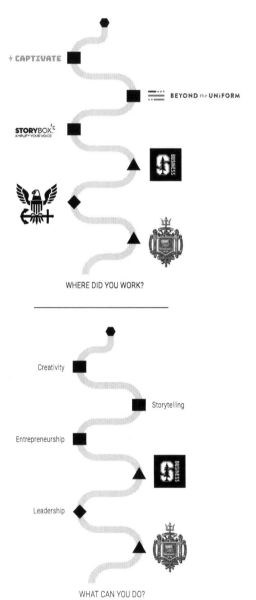

WHERE DID YOU WORK?

_____

WHAT CAN YOU DO?

CHAPTER SEVEN

LOREN COHEN: FROM LAWYER TO JOB TRAINING ENTREPRENEUR

In December 2020, Laura White, a former colleague of mine from Ashoka, posted on LinkedIn that she learned the facets of strategy and business operations through an immersive, project-based program called Skillful. Given that business operations is my forte, I researched Skillful, going so far as to complete an online form to become a mentor in the program. That action led me to a virtual conversation with the cofounder and CEO, Loren Cohen. She followed a nontraditional path: corporate lawyer turned entrepreneur, helping others to find success in nontechnical roles in technology companies.

Cohen grew up surrounded by stories of business, listening to her late father share the successes of the private equity venture capital firm he founded. She recalled family dinners and weekly lunches with him, where business concepts were the main topic. This dialogue informed her decision to study business at McGill University. She reflected on this decision,

sharing, "I always loved business, but"—she quickly inter-
jects—"none of the structured career paths out of business
school excited me." Cohen explored college internships to
better understand different work environments. "My summer
internships were not good reference points for a business
career."

A chance conversation on a family vacation opened her eyes
to the legal industry. A family friend was a commercial liti-
gator, who described his job as fast-paced, involving constant
exposure to new concepts and working with smart people.
Cohen became intrigued by the challenging work environment of a law firm, especially since she enjoyed reading. She
not only studied for the law school admission test (LSAT),
but she also secured an internship in a small boutique law
firm. The experience helped her visualize how she would fit
into a law firm: "I can see myself doing law for a little while.
The work seemed interesting enough. My goal in the long
term was to be a founder and entrepreneur."

Cohen went straight from college to law school at the University of Toronto in fall 2013. She described law school as
"an amazing way to learn how to think and how to learn."
She practiced foundational legal concepts, including a "ratio,"
where she read a complicated fifty-page legal case from hundreds of years ago, then distilled down the point of law for
her classwork. Cohen also developed her written communication skills.

Cohen hit her stride early in law school as she was one of a
handful of students selected to join Goodmans LLP, a transaction law firm specializing in business law and litigation, in

both summer 2014 and 2015. Then, she received an offer to join them in a full-time capacity as an associate in fall 2016. As a services professional, Cohen became more efficient in her interactions to manage up, with difficult stakeholders both inside and outside of the law firm. However, she plotted her future by considering her Goodmans experience as "a great place to start your career and learn base-level skills that could be applied to a whole host of different things."

By January 2019, the Goodmans associates were starting to specialize in an area of law. The idea of specializing did not appeal to Cohen. She preferred the day-to-day tasks of an associate that challenged her to learn about a new client or topic. She felt, "I've gotten the core skill set from law, and now, it's time to move on. I knew that my second step would be entrepreneurial. For me to bridge that gap confidently, I knew that there was an in-between step of actually being boots on the ground at a business."

Cohen scheduled fifteen to twenty informational interviews with other Toronto lawyers that left the legal profession in spring 2019. While business networking was not comfortable, she challenged herself to reach out to at least five people per week and have two conversations per week. She found them through word of mouth, podcasts, LinkedIn, and a blog which featured lawyers who transitioned into technology. From her conversations, she concluded, "The best way for me to maintain that generalist skill set in a different context that challenges me and exposes me to a new industry and roles would be working at a very early-stage startup, where you can touch a bunch of different functional areas that are interesting."

Cohen decided to optimize for personal growth, not salary or security, by joining an early-stage startup. She recounts, "This felt like, both personally and professionally the right time of my life to take a risk." Through her conversations, she came across Shift, a software that helps companies with their organizational culture, where the progressive founders were former management consultants. With a shared understanding as services professionals, they understood how a lawyer could be an asset to their budding team, so they hired Cohen to focus on general company operations.

Cohen cultivated a strong relationship with her manager, who was the head of sales and operations. Since the company was small, she would identify an interesting project and let her manager know she wanted to work on it. Cohen remembers those interactions fondly, commenting, "Every quarter, we would carve out new things for me to get my hands on and learn." For example, she expressed an interest in the talent acquisition process, so she studied it from start to finish when they were hiring a head of product, by working alongside the recruiters interviewing and evaluating fifty of the best candidates from across North America. "It was an amazing way for me to understand different roles." Cohen expanded her duties to include people operations, then ultimately, the entire human resources function within the first year.

Sixteen months into the role, Cohen felt "the startup bug started to call me." Shift was on shaky ground as the COVID-19 pandemic impacted its clients. She highlighted that "everything was so uncertain," but steadfastly said, "I felt the growth trajectory of the company changed and therefore, my personal growth with it."

During the past two years, Cohen stayed in touch with Kris Lachance, a lawyer that had transitioned from a law firm into the startup world a few months ahead of her. Lachance explored the future of work in his then role as entrepreneur-in-residence at Real Ventures, which invested in early-stage technology startups.

Given that both of them were now part of this small group of Toronto-based lawyers no longer practicing, they continued to receive outreach about their career transitions, and held conversations with each other about career paths into the technology sector. Between the two of them, they estimated speaking to one hundred individuals from Toronto that wanted to pivot careers like they did across a two-year span. Over four months, these conversations between them evolved into a startup idea: "There's a big market of helping business professionals' level up or make their next career move. Everyone's focused on engineers and technical roles, but no one's paying attention to the rest of the pie, which are the business roles." They closed the loop on their research by speaking to people who worked at technology startups to understand their careers. May 2020 proved to be the right time for both of them to leave their jobs and work together as cofounders launching Skillful, a job training program, into a viable business. They followed the Lean Startup methodology, with two key tenants: "Let's build something people want and let's test that immediately."

Within five weeks, Cohen and Lachance spoke to a variety of strategy and business operations professionals at local technology companies to understand what their day-to-day activities were, then reverse-engineered a curriculum. Then, they reached back out to the most engaging individuals for help in creating a simulation project for the students and designated them as mentors. The mentors brought a complementary viewpoint to their own, given that they worked in business operations roles in technology companies. Their ask to the mentors was straightforward: "Do you want to help us cocreate a project that will help people basically simulate what a typical business operations project is like at your company? Through that, the students will learn skills in a very applied, hands-on way."

Their experiment worked as Cohen reflected on the teamwork effort: "We ended up cocreating it with the mentors. It's really based on the idea that we wanted to build a skills-training program that actually emulates what you do on the job and then, you're being taught from people who actually have the job you want." In the first year, Cohen and Lachance graduated almost three hundred business professionals, divided into ten six-week cohorts under the guidance of over twenty-five mentors. The cohort structure ensured completion rates are high: "You're accountable to a team and mentor as part of your cohort. It's a shared learning experience. It's a low-risk way to trial and error a project before making a big decision like saying yes or no to a new job or changing industries."

Cohen is quick to flag that breaking into a new industry was not easy—not only from her own personal experience, but from the couple hundred people she connected with trying to do the same. She advised, "Even though it's uncomfortable to network or break into a community, finding people to deeply connect with who are going through something similar or who have gone through something similar to coach you through it will have an outsize impact on your career trajectory." Cohen described business networking as "a muscle that you have to strengthen. Everyone was willing to chat with me because we have a shared experience and background and they went through a career transition."

When Cohen and Lachance took the risk to launch Skillful during a pandemic, they put their fears of failure aside to create an opportunity for others to learn the skills necessary to thrive in technology companies. Regina Dugan tied together defying the impossible and refusing the fear of failure in her 2012 TED talk, revealing, "These two ideas are connected more than you may realize, because when you remove the fear of failure, impossible things suddenly become possible... I'm not encouraging failure; I'm discouraging fear of failure."

Cohen's Key Skills:

- Curiosity, which helped Cohen meet others to understand her career options and help others discover a path into technology companies.
- Discipline, which Cohen used to further her knowledge of her client work and setting up her business through research.
- Proactiveness, which Cohen and Lachance demonstrated as they solidified, vetted, and launched their startup proof of concept.

Cohen also encouraged, "If you don't have a certain skill, just get out there and do it. That will make every time you apply for a job easier." It reminds me of her taking the chance with the college internship at the boutique law firm to see if she would enjoy both being a lawyer and the experience of working at a law firm.

Loren Cohen

Skillful

✎ shift

Goodmans

🛡 UNIVERSITY OF TORONTO LAW

🛡 McGill UNIVERSITY

WHERE DID YOU WORK?

Entrepreneurship

Business operations

Law

🛡 UNIVERSITY OF TORONTO LAW

🛡 McGill UNIVERSITY

WHAT CAN YOU DO?

CHAPTER EIGHT

WASSIM MATAR: FROM ENGINEER TO VENTURE CAPITALIST

When I pursued my MBA, I had a singular focus: to pivot my career back into the private sector. Half of my MIT Sloan Fellows classmates faced imminent return to their sponsoring companies, but the rest came in with their eyes wide open of what could happen next.

Four months into my degree, I met Wassim Matar, a classmate with a background in the transportation industry with roots in Europe, the Middle East, and North Africa. We quickly became friends working together as two of the five cofounders of a startup called Pirca, which aimed to solve Latin American transportation congestion issues through carpool optimization. He was our go-to person for modeling traffic patterns.

For Matar, his Pirca contribution was an extension of his professional experience of ten years designing transportation systems as a lead transport planner at Dar Group, a Beirut-based consulting firm focused on sustainable advancement of communities. Prior to that experience, he completed back-to-back undergraduate and master's engineering degrees at University College London and Imperial College London with a specialty in transportation and urban design. He applied these concepts to his consulting work, including the Muscat area traffic study model.

Matar led a sixty-person team formulating a thirty-year master city plan for Muscat, Oman in 2010. While envisioning a city of the future, he examined "different analytical data sets, including the existing road networks and land uses, economic projections, and population projections to shape a phased proposal that expanded existing roads, added transportation hubs, and incorporated a light-rail system. I learned to make these large master plans, taking huge leaps of faith anchored in analytical data." While their proposals were grounded in the reality of the citizens using this infrastructure, Matar's team had to please the client: "The stakeholder was every single governmental body. Everybody has a stake in what their city is going to be and you have to manage their input." He learned to anticipate challenges to the plans and mitigate the risks surfaced by the clients.

Back in Cambridge, MA, our Pirca team explored the entrepreneurial ecosystem across MIT, including our participation in the Sandbox Innovation Fund and class projects for Scaling New Ventures, Competitive Strategy, and X-Lab. We took our primary research seriously, reaching out to the people with similar experience in larger companies such as Google and venture capitalists that funded this type of endeavor. With the exception of one marketplace entrepreneur, who we found out was in the process of a large fundraising round when we reached out, we met with everyone we contacted that academic year. Our Pirca experience demonstrated how we could manifest and test a startup idea into reality in months.

When I implored him to join me for the second class in Money for Startups, Matar was game. MIT's mechanical engineering program offered this class to provide students with the frameworks for how entrepreneurs and founders of startups raised money to build their companies. Week after week, senior lecturer Shari Loessberg invited venture capitalists to share case studies of their investment processes. Among a handful of business school students in the room, we gained exposure to how the engineering students approached the issues. For Matar, it was vernacular he was familiar with, having spent his entire career as an engineer. We sat in the front row of the class absorbing the practices of these leading investors, putting them into practice with Pirca. Smitten with their stories, Matar figured out his career pivot.

"It was the combination of the classes, the classmates, and trying out different things," Matar explained, describing how this collective learning process opened his eyes to an entirely new ecosystem of possibility. With these limited experiences in entrepreneurship at MIT, following graduation in June 2017, Matar created his own venture capital (VC) fund called Verve Ventures. When I questioned the risk involved, he described his mindset as, "After leaving MIT, you're in this cloud of Americana. You can do anything; you're walking on water and just gliding. Everything you touch turns to gold." As someone who was initially skeptical of the MBA curriculum, he went on to say, "MIT is an ecosystem of amazing ideas." He used to believe technical expertise underpinned an idea 99 percent of the time, but he now learned there were additional factors leading to an idea's success: team and execution.

As Matar created Verve Ventures, researched portfolio companies, found investors, and brought on an advisory team, he identified similarities to his previous engineering experiences. "In engineering, you are trying to see how a building will break or fall [to avoid poor infrastructure], whereas the venture capitalist takes the opposite approach, in seeing how you can make a company stand with very little foundation." He found a happy medium in building a portfolio of deep technology (deep tech) startups, where the technical expertise needs to be defensible because it must solve a substantial scientific challenge and the team and culture must be strong enough to weather the storm to demonstrate success. This combination is important because deep technology investments have a longer runway for their return on investment than traditional investments.

As Matar solidified his approach, he also needed to find willing investors to fund the selected deep tech companies in his portfolio. In the first ten years of his career, he built up his Rolodex of people across the Middle East and Africa, describing it as "planting seeds, so you can enjoy the shade later—at some point, I could go back to them." He began an iterative process of outreach for Verve Ventures, where he rebuilt relationships with potentially larger investors, then refined his elevator pitch until they signed with him.

Finally, Matar realized while his expertise in transportation and mobility were sound, he could not perform the same level of due diligence on some of the other types of emerging technologies used by portfolio companies. He sought to create a bench of advisors, including myself, our classmates including Ana Maria Gomez Lopez, Alan Hanley, and Bruno Nogueira, and senior lecturer Loessberg, who could step in to perform the necessary due diligence and provide recommendations on a firm's potential. He also found investors have more confidence in Verve because of the extended team.

I had the chance to tag along to a meeting to evaluate a potential portfolio company in October 2019, back at our old stomping grounds at MIT Sloan. In one of the study rooms, we met Dipanwita Das, the founder and CEO of a startup called Sorcero. Sorcero is a software that uses artificial intelligence (AI) and natural language processing technologies to surface relevant documents needed at life sciences companies. After Matar and Das discussed the team structure and current clients, he stepped back from the discussion. I took over, starting with a commonality—I asked about her previous work in a social enterprise in Washington, DC, then dove into the technical aspects with her to better understand how the startup delivers on its capabilities to the customers. After our meeting, I remember asking if it was fine that I took over that part of the meeting. I did not know he was not at all familiar with these technologies. He grinned, saying, "This is the reason I want more and more people involved to complement my knowledge and skillset." Our teamwork on the due diligence resulted in an investment from Verve Ventures in Sorcero.

Matar continues to find ways to reinforce the model that is Verve Ventures by iterating on its investing approach for its second round of investment and discovering a new type of investor, a second-generation member in a family business, to be part of his extended team. He found the second-generation family member was likely to add venture capital investing in their family office portfolio but did not know how to do so. Matar found an opportunity to mentor them with a "VC-as-a-Service" offering. This shift in investor profile would also create long-lasting relationships that could bring in subsequent investments.

Matar's openness to learning about entrepreneurship and the risks involved in setting up a new venture defined his shift into venture capital. In making the career pivot, he relied on the newfound credibility, confidence, and teamwork he discovered in the MBA. He also became aware that his own vulnerability could guide him to those with more knowledge.

Vulnerability is something Harvard Business School professor Rosabeth Moss Kanter inspired in her 2013 TED talk. She empowered the audience to "show up, speak up, look up, team up, never give up, and lift others up."

Matar embodies the aspects of Kanter's six ways to lead positive change. He showed up to the MIT programming that opened his eyes to a new industry, spoke up to ask his professional network to fund his venture, looked up to align his investments in deep tech solutions with long-term impact, teamed up with experts to select the investments, never gave up when he hit a bump in the road on the first fund, and lifted others up in his advisory structure.

Matar's Key Skills:

- Complex problem solving, which Matar developed as an engineer, then applied to building his own venture.
- Team building, which Matar was familiar with from the transportation consulting projects but flexed as he brought in different levels of advisors into his VC fund.
- Vulnerability, which Matar displayed as he sold his new business idea to professional contacts from his previous career.

Matar innately knew the importance of a strong team as he moved from project to project across the Middle East. He amassed those contacts without knowing when he would dip into the well of water. I observed that he waited for the right moment to engage them, in this case to fund Verve Ventures, with the right talk track that kept them engaged.

Wassim Matar

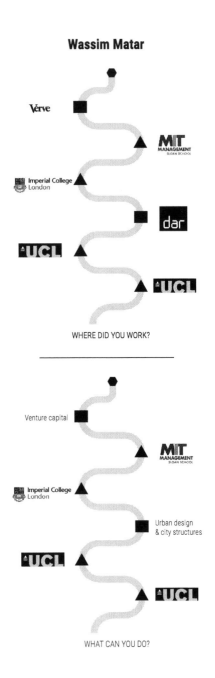

Vérve

MIT MANAGEMENT SLOAN SCHOOL

Imperial College London

dar

UCL

UCL

WHERE DID YOU WORK?

Venture capital

MIT MANAGEMENT SLOAN SCHOOL

Imperial College London

Urban design
& city structures

UCL

UCL

WHAT CAN YOU DO?

MARKETING

CHAPTER NINE

LINDSEY LYNES: FROM COORDINATOR TO CLIENT SERVICES EXECUTIVE

When I moved to New York in March 2018, I wanted to grow my professional network by joining a private club or group that curated like-minded individuals. I had success with a similar decision in Buenos Aires by joining a private club called The Clubhouse, where I became friends with other expatriates and startup founders. In early 2019, I discovered Chief, a private network focused on connecting and supporting women executives. Similar to The Clubhouse, Chief offered a physical location, but also extensive programming and executive coaching as part of its annual membership fee. As part of the experience, they assigned us to a "core group" composed of eight to twelve women around our age to discuss leadership challenges and frameworks. In this core group, I met Lindsey Lynes.

Lynes found Chief through a LinkedIn post in early 2020, during her relocation from Atlanta, GA, to Old Greenwich, CT. While she migrated up the East Coast for work before, she stated, "It was hard to create a natural professional network in a new city. I wanted to put more intention in my leadership practice and have the support of mentors and peers outside of my company. In reading about the purpose and mission of Chief, it resonated so clearly to me."

Lynes's first full-time job upon graduating from the University of Georgia in spring 2005 was as Brown Bag Marketing's seventh hire, taking the role of administrative assistant to the CEO Doug Brown. She quickly became the go-getter in the office during her sixteen-year tenure with the marketing agency. Her willingness to raise her hand at every opportunity came from her mentality of "if not me, then who?" Lynes described it as, "It's an instinct. If there's a ball in the field, you don't have to wonder who's going to get the ball. I'm going to grab it." She drew the parallel to our core group, where "if the executive coach asks a question and no one answers, I can't handle it not to say something." Brown believed in her capabilities early on and trusted Lynes with projects.

Lynes spent most of her time working with clients on the account management team. She thrived on the office culture of "late nights, creativity, and wild-brain ideas." She began monthly one-on-one meetings with Mark Pugh, the chief of staff. Lynes respected Pugh's leadership style, diction, and command of situations. From him, she learned the importance of being thoughtful and intentional in her leadership practice. She took mental notes on his methods that she filed away for her own future use.

Eight years into her career, she received an opportunity to work in house with a major customer in Hoboken, New Jersey, developing her relationship management expertise from a different angle. At one point, the customer approached Lynes and Brown Bag Marketing about expanding the responsibility to include their loyalty and rebate marketing program. While it was not an area Lynes or her teammates were familiar with, she raised her hand. With a startup mindset, she figured out how to set up a rebate program. The pilot was so successful, Brown Bag Marketing set up a sister company called Vetlocity, dedicated to loyalty and reward programs, and unleashed Lynes to run it as their director of business operations.

Lynes returned to Brown Bag's headquarters, where she could rely on a brain trust of the collective employees to develop Vetlocity. She pulled together existing colleagues and hired new ones. Lynes found a knack for identifying the right talent at the right time. She also invested in her people management capabilities by learning how to position the new roles as professional development opportunities for the colleagues she wanted to bring over to the venture. Lynes and her ten-person team grew Vetlocity to be a five-million-dollar business over three years.

Lynes enjoyed the talent responsibilities so much that when Brown Bag's human resources (HR) manager left the organization in September 2016, she raised her hand to serve as the interim HR manager until a new one joined. After a few months of balancing both roles, she negotiated to take the HR role full time as a vice president of people and culture. Two years later, when the controller left the company, she raised her hand again to take on expanded financial responsibility as a vice president of operations. In this newly created role in August 2018, she brought together the HR and finance teams under her purview to better provide the executives with holistic visibility into the company's projects and metrics, as she did at Vetlocity.

Over a year after working the newly-formed role overseeing Brown Bag's operations, the company went through major restructuring under new ownership and Lynes found herself back in account management on a major customer in New Jersey, but without having to relocate to their offices again. Once again, she relied on her trusted teammates to join her on the account team responsible for this large client. While it had been seven years and three tours of duty within Brown Bag, Lynes was ready to approach the customer's marketing challenges with a new lens from running the operations of two businesses, steering digital campaigns, and informing others through analytical insights. She noted, "I'm such a better marketer now than I was." Her perspective on the different components of running a business has given her a broader outlook. As Lynes described, "It made my thinking go from a square to a cube." Her tenacity led to her most recent promotion of senior vice president of client services.

Lynes's willingness to raise her hand in any situation is unflappable. She made major career shifts in her areas of responsibility within the same company. She recognized, "Every job I've ever had has made me better at every other job I've had."

Lynes displayed what Kare Anderson in her famous TED talk from September 2014 calls "opportunity makers." She detailed the three traits of opportunity-makers as, "Opportunity-makers keep honing their top strength and they become pattern seekers. They get involved in different worlds than their worlds so they're trusted and they can see those patterns, and they communicate to connect around sweet spots of shared interest." Lynes exemplified the opportunity maker Anderson described. As a marketer, she knew how to work well with customers and what the business needed to succeed. She studied those patterns from various angles as she rotated through different roles during her tenure and took her findings to the other executives. Anderson goes on to say, "Opportunity-makers are actively seeking situations with people unlike them, and they're building relationships, and because they do that, they have trusted relationships where they can bring the right team in and recruit them to solve a problem better and faster and seize more opportunities." When Lynes was in troubleshooting mode, she had many colleagues she could rely on to help her.

Lynes's Key Skills:

- Dependability, which she and Brown Bag Marketing's leadership relied on to broaden her scope of responsibilities.
- Open-mindedness, which Lynes demonstrated in taking on projects or relocating to work closely with the customer.
- People management, which Lynes exhibited in assembling the Vetlocity team.

Lynes sought to challenge herself by accepting increasing responsibility in her career. The trust she built with her superiors gave her a runway to reimagine the work as her own. Her story demonstrates how you can continue to thrive within an organization you enjoy working in.

Lindsey Lynes

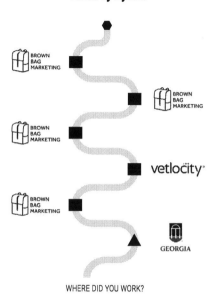

BROWN BAG MARKETING

BROWN BAG MARKETING

BROWN BAG MARKETING

vetlocity

BROWN BAG MARKETING

GEORGIA

WHERE DID YOU WORK?

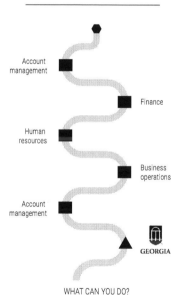

Account management

Finance

Human resources

Business operations

Account management

GEORGIA

WHAT CAN YOU DO?

CHAPTER TEN

CARTER HOLLAND: FROM GUITARIST TO CORPORATE MARKETER

———

Carter Holland joined the executive team as the interim chief marketing officer at Sprinklr in fall 2020. While he brought in the tried-and-true marketing frameworks that helped his previous technology employers succeed, no one imagined the toolkit he developed as a musician. Let's dig into his repertoire.

Holland picked up the trumpet at seven years old. His passion for music became stronger as he learned how to play more instruments, mainly the guitar in middle school. He channeled this energy into a gap year after high school by participating in Up with People, a one-year long program involving performing arts, community service, and travel, where he could show off his craft by performing in the group's roadshows.

On this whirlwind tour in 1986, he plotted his next steps: "I ultimately decided to go to college to get a degree that was not in music. I needed to have something to fall back on. It was a safety net." So, Holland honed his art at Denison University, majoring in English composition because of his innate gift for writing. All the while, he played the guitar in rock bands during college and, subsequently, the same during his return home to New Jersey.

During this post-college phase, Holland sought some stability by delivering private guitar lessons to high school students. He also took the lead in managing aspects of the different bands he played with, by booking the venues, negotiating pay rates, and designing promotional materials. He continued to market himself as a solo artist and developed a thick skin as he received critiques of his sample music demos. Finally, he deepened his improvisational techniques as he applied jazz elements to the rock songs he performed repeatedly with different bands. The experimentation meant the same songs never sounded the same twice! He was an entrepreneur but never contemplated the word during this time, reflecting, "As an artist, you are always trying to come up with something original and different. I didn't think of my work as a product; I thought of it as art." For six years, Holland juggled the hand-to-mouth nature of tutoring and band gigs, which eventually took their toll.

As Holland contemplated ending his sixteen-year music journey in spring 1995, he received an introduction to Paul Verna, a reviews editor at *Billboard Magazine*, through a friend of a friend of his parents. At the time, *Billboard Magazine* was (and still is) one of the world's most influential music media brands. Holland shared a demo of his original music, hoping for insights to extend his music career. Instead, because Verna liked to hire "musicians who could also write," it resulted in a freelance journalist role—a new avenue to explore that offered a regular paycheck.

Holland used the opportunity to move from New York City to Boston for a fresh start as he continued to write for *Billboard Magazine* and compose songs of his own. His older sister, Lynda, introduced him to people she knew in his neighborhood, including Steve Bookbinder, a senior executive in the organizational change management and communications practice of Towers Perrin (now called Willis Towers Watson), a human resources management consulting firm. Bookbinder's firm hired writers. So, when Bookbinder learned Holland wrote articles for *Billboard Magazine*, he administered a short writing test to Holland, which showed he was a good fit for the openings in their communication practice. Starting in fall 1996, Holland began his climb up corporate America.

While Holland navigated an office environment for the first time, he knew he needed to catch up salary wise with his peers that joined the firm right out of university, sometimes making double what he did because they had graduate degrees. He recapped the moment he talked to management: "I basically said to them, 'I need to fast track my career here. I want to do more.'" Holland's willingness to advocate for himself resulted in more responsibility (and the requisite salary) as he became more involved with other projects in the organizational research and change management practice areas.

Holland also found that by trading his song sheets for PowerPoint slides, he could translate his ability to perform on stage to present in conference rooms. The management team took notice of this double threat. Using his solid writing and stage presence as an asset, they brought Holland to client meetings. In one of these first instances, Holland worked alongside Bookbinder on a change management strategy for a five-hundred-million-dollar manufacturing company, when Bookbinder said, "I want you to present the data, instead of me," as they entered a boardroom with three C-level executives. With this trust, Holland enjoyed presenting research findings and recommendations to clients.

After four years of rising up the ranks at Towers Perrin and working with different clients, Holland realized his creative passions could find a better outlet in the corporate function of marketing. He started a job hunt that focused on marketing roles at music technology companies in Boston to combine his interests. His wife, Amy, discovered Avid, a film and video editing software company that also had a division at the forefront of digital audio technology. Holland's research found Avid had recently completed a corporate restructuring, which created an internal communications manager role in their marketing department. The premise of the role was writing and to work closely with the CEO and other Avid executives to articulate the company's new narrative. This angle proved to be an in-house version of what Holland learned to do as a management consultant at Towers Perrin, so he took the role and developed it into an eleven-year marketing career at Avid. A few years in, he hired Verna to join his corporate communications team.

In his new career as a marketer, Holland relied on his writing capability to explain the story of the company through executive speeches, press releases, and investor relations presentations. He also began to see patterns between his ability to improvise musically and the continuous improvement cycles within business. He summarizes this observation: "In business, you're always optimizing. You're always thinking about why did that event or program work well, what didn't work well, and how are we going to do it again to take it to the next level. I'm kind of relentless about it. I'm never satisfied with the way we did it, almost to a fault. I always want to find new ways to deliver better results and that is often what drives success in the business world." And prolific he has been, Holland's taken on the senior executive role of chief marketing officer in three other software technology companies in the last decade.

Holland's creativity was present in his different roles. Musician turned entrepreneur Jeb Banner hired other musicians in his businesses, sharing an emerging pattern at his 2013 TED talk: "I noticed over time bands were really startups and that musicians were really entrepreneurs. When you're in a band, you have to learn a lot about business. You have to learn about branding, how to name yourself, marketing, how to take yourself to market. Though they may look very different, but a band, it looks a lot like a business—like a startup." Banner's sentiment validated Holland's own feelings on the topic.

Banner goes on to state, "Bands serve the music and they take it to market. They go out and they get people to buy those CDs or download those tracks. Go play those songs; play those songs for people. That's why you see so many musicians in marketing and advertising. It's natural to them." Banner believed musicians naturally bring in teamwork, creativity, and purpose to business, which can help a business to grow.

Holland's Key Skills:

- Continuous improvement, which Holland picked up as improvisation in his music gigs and later encouraged his marketing teams to embrace in their initiatives.
- Performing, which Holland learned at a young age, then applied to his management consultant role in delivering client presentations.
- Storytelling, which Holland formulated as a songwriter, then used in professional roles to explain or revise corporate narratives to please the stakeholders.

Holland's mastery of his key skills shined to those that brought him out of the music world. Holland acknowledged, "When I was a musician, I would not have been able to articulate my skills as things that would help me in the business world." I find that while he definitely reinvented himself, he stayed true to his strengths and passions in pulling himself up the career ladder.

Carter Holland

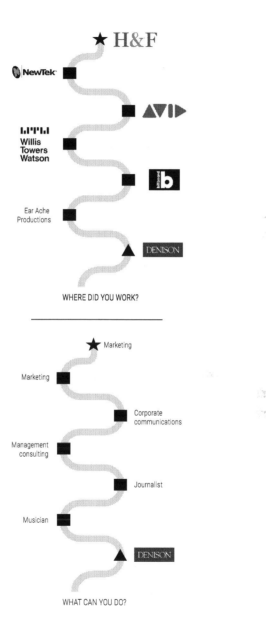

★ H&F

NewTek ■

AVI▶

Willis
Towers
Watson ■

■ b

Ear Ache
Productions ■

▲ DENISON

WHERE DID YOU WORK?

★ Marketing

Marketing ■

■ Corporate
communications

Management
consulting ■

■ Journalist

Musician ■

▲ DENISON

WHAT CAN YOU DO?

CHAPTER ELEVEN

MICHELLE UDEZUE: FROM ACCOUNTANT TO BRAND MARKETER

———

In January 2015, I met Michelle Udezue at the Forté MBA Launch kick-off event in Reston, Virginia. Assigned to the same small group of MBA candidates in a ten-month program, we traded introductions, where I learned Udezue was an accountant determined to be a marketer. This drastic career change always piqued my interest. In Udezue's case, her international upbringing guided her choices for school and work.

Udezue grew up in Nigeria and arrived at the University of Massachusetts Amherst at the age of fifteen to start her undergraduate studies in fall 2001. Her intention to major in psychology was fraught with concern over the viability of a career as a psychologist in Nigeria. She believed "if you studied economics, you became an economist, if you studied math, you were a mathematician, so with psychology, obviously, I'm going to be a psychologist." Then, she continued, "I wasn't sure where I wanted to be after graduation—like did I want to stay in the US or go back to Nigeria? Nigerians don't go to psychologists, so that meant I couldn't go back with this degree." Her narrow view was not uncommon, especially as she did not talk about career options with anyone outside of her immediate family.

Udezue ended up double majoring in marketing and communications, keeping psychology as her minor. Given the school was in a suburban college town and she was so young, Udezue said when it came to looking for internships, "I felt like the school was so big and never wondered what was outside of it." She took classes year round, with a few extracurricular activities including theater and Upward Bound rounding out her studies.

As graduation approached in spring 2005, she mailed cover letters and resumes to advertising agencies in New York City for full-time roles, with no luck. Udezue met a handful of financial institutions through on-campus recruiting, who pitched the role of personal financial advisors to the marketing majors. "They talked about how you can use your marketing skills because you are selling to people. I had never thought about this career, and it sounded interesting to me," Udezue described. She accepted her first job as a financial advisor with a Connecticut-based firm, Waddell & Reed. The company required its financial advisors to carry certain certifications, so she purchased the study guides and prepared for the Series 7 exam for the first few months. "Context is everything," Udezue responded to me as my eyes widened at her accomplishment. "I didn't know that these exams are supposed to be hard. For me, it was like taking any other class—read the book, take the practice quizzes, then complete the exam. Later on, I found out that people view it as a difficult exam."

During this time, Udezue learned more about the financial services company and the role: "I was very adamant that I didn't want to do cold calling, so they presented these other options like attending job fairs or community college classes to find warm leads, but I had to pay the out-of-pocket expenses. It was like running your own business. Then, I started to think, 'Who's going to take financial advice from a nineteen-year-old?'" Udezue looked for a new job, with a college friend recommending another financial services firm called State Street in Boston, MA.

State Street onboarded batches of new hires based on ability and taught accounting concepts to them, which Udezue was familiar with from her Amherst days. However, after one and half months, she felt the work was rote and asked her manager for stretch projects. She also attended seminars in Boston, where she learned to "think about what you want to do by looking for job postings that you may be interested in the future. See what the requirements are like, then you can work towards them." Udezue's cursory search of accounting roles surfaced the common requirement of a Certified Public Account (CPA) license, which became her new career goal. She needed more academic credits to qualify, so she left her job to enroll full time at Suffolk University in fall 2006 to earn her master's in accounting.

In the Suffolk University hallways, Udezue learned about the "big four" accounting firms, a nickname for Deloitte, Ernst & Young, KPMG, and PwC, settling on PwC as "the one where I wanted to work." She applied for jobs but did not hear back on interviews. Then, she remembered she could access the Amherst job board as an alumna. When she saw PwC posted dates for on-campus recruiting, Udezue drove one and a half hours from Boston to Amherst for a chance to meet their representative. Her long shot paid off as she recalled, "The recruiter was blown away, describing my initiative [as] 'you don't even go to school here, you just wanted to meet me,' then put me straight into an interview process for a summer internship."

Udezue also figured out why she did not get any interviews through her earlier applications. "It was the same resume that I submitted via Suffolk and Amherst, but applying through Suffolk did not serve me well. Suffolk was not a target school for the Big Four, so they had a few hiring slots for many Suffolk candidates. The more reputable Amherst was the feeder program funneling more candidates to the Big Four firms."

Following her PwC internship and graduation from Suffolk, Udezue studied for and passed the CPA license exam. She also took some time for herself by taking a French language immersion course in spring 2008. She negotiated a full-time offer with PwC to join their New York City tax practice that fall. The management consulting lifestyle took its toll on Udezue, where she felt "I didn't own my life or my time. I didn't mind the work, but really hated the hours."

In her second year, Udezue participated in a training she described as "life changing." An outside consultant administered the Myers-Brigg Type Indicator (MBTI) assessment to her cohort, where the results showed the cohort predominantly fell into two adjacent of the sixteen types. Udezue was the only one who had a different MBTI type, which was the polar opposite of the rest of the group. She reflected on how the instructor pulled her aside to acknowledge the difference, where she noted, "I won't be able to change the company culture to suit me, so maybe it's not a good fit for my personality type." She now had the words to describe her feelings toward work and understand why she moved at a different pace than her peers.

"I actually did like tax, but I didn't like the lifestyle," Udezue admitted, channeling these insights into a new job search. An online search introduced her to federal government roles, where she saw positions at the Internal Revenue Service and a chance to work closer to the actual tax law, which interested her. The lifestyle was also more her speed. Udezue joined a specialized group for excise tax in 2010, which worried her after a few months. She considered the exit options, which were far limited because of the narrow applicability: "I felt no one is looking for excise tax services outside of the IRS."

She cut the internal debate short when an unexpected trip home to Nigeria prompted her to consider her options. Udezue said, "I didn't want to keep going down this path with the IRS. I wanted to move back to Nigeria and complete my youth service." Nigeria's national service year was compulsory for college graduates, serving as a requirement for any employment. Since returning to Nigeria was always in the back of Udezue's mind, it was the right time to complete the program.

In 2011, Udezue packed up her belongings for her move home to Nigeria. Given the broad scope for the National Youth Service Corps programming, she strived for a marketing opportunity. Through her father, she met with the local representative of the global communications firm Saatchi & Saatchi, but did not like the office atmosphere. Through a high school friend, she met with an on-air radio personality at Silverbird Communications, who oversaw their radio stations. Udezue took the meeting hoping he could connect her with the team at their sister company called Silverbird Productions so she could find an advertising or event planning opportunity. He advised her, "I can introduce you to someone on the event side, but I don't know what will happen. Have you ever thought about radio?" With his purview over the radio stations, she could work for Silverbird in a role that met the service program's requirements.

Udezue spent her first three days as a news broadcaster before audience complaints about her American accent forced management to reassign her. She switched to a morning show and did not mind the change from scripted to live commentary. After the program aired, she studied the radio station's landscape. Despite the fact that Silverbird had the larger market share of advertising dollars due to its reach, the social capital shifted towards newer radio stations that leveraged social media and influencers to grow their name. When Udezue raised her concerns about the radio station's lack of social media presence to management, they responded with, "You can be in charge of social media." She used the opportunity to set up social media accounts for each state, and as a result, she provided new avenues for the on-air personalities to engage with their opinionated audience.

Udezue referenced her marketing knowledge from her college days to advance the radio's sphere of influence. She also recognized a new feeling: "I became very much aware of what it feels like when you actually care about your job. I would leave work and think about ways that we could do something better. I never had that thought at work before." For her, it confirmed she needed to work in a more creative space. She explored an exciting opportunity with a new music television station, but the unpaid nature caused her to re-evaluate her personal situation—she had student loans.

Realistic, and aiming for the bigger picture, Udezue returned to the US to secure an accounting job to pay off her debts. She joined Cherry-Bekaert LLP, a small accounting firm in Virginia, as a senior tax accountant in spring 2012. Unexpectedly, the team experienced full turnover and she had to train two other new hires. The long hours reminded her of her consulting days.

Udezue researched what it would take to switch into a marketing or entertainment career to fuel her creativity. She looked at graduate degree programs in marketing, but at programs' open houses, she discovered "most of the professionals completing the specialty master's degree already worked in marketing, then leveraged their connections to find a new job." Given she was new to the DC area, she did not have a network to lean on. This option would not be successful.

Udezue saw her friends completing MBAs and meeting companies during on-campus recruiting events. She remembered her own experience meeting with PwC. She reasoned,

"Business school would provide a level-playing field of opportunities." As she made her target school list, she focused on which schools attracted the employers she cared about. In spring 2014, she set her sights on enrolling in business school in fall 2015. After the busy tax season finished, she paralleled eleven business school applications and the Forté MBA Launch program application to increase her chances.

This is where our paths crossed, through the Forté MBA Launch program. During our conversation, I saw how our first few months were wildly different. While the rest of the group studied for the GMAT and began assembling their target school list, Udezue was off visiting seven schools during their admission weekends to see if she liked the academic environment.

By summer, Udezue enrolled in Northwestern University's Kellogg School of Management, renowned for its marketing programming. She participated in student life, taking an active role with the Media and Entertainment Club. By her spring semester, she realized, "Most media and entertainment companies hired MBA candidates to work in finance functions, like mergers and acquisitions or business development. I wanted to be on the creative side."

This frustrated Udezue, because she did not see marketing roles that interested her, yet she kept an open mind about the companies visiting campus. She snagged an open interview slot for a buyer role with Target, represented by a Kellogg alumna that was the former vice president of entertainment. Udezue had no idea what a buyer did. She listened to the executive explain her work: "When Beyoncé released her surprise album at Target, it had ripple effects across the stores. On the buying side, you get to work with all of the record labels because they want placement in the stores." During their conversation, Udezue's interest in the role grew: "I never really thought about what buyers do. Originally, I looked at the record labels for a job, but on the buying side, I could see how all of them run their different businesses. Instead of going to one and learning one's business, I could learn from many record labels. I was excited about the opportunity."

In summer 2016, Udezue joined the buyer intern program at Target's headquarters in Minneapolis, MN. She landed a spot with the beauty team but said, "I was upset because I wanted to be in entertainment, specifically music." Soon she learned beauty is in tune with pop culture, so entertainment aspects were mixed into her job. Udezue enjoyed working in a different company culture than her previous employers. As with most MBA internships, she received a full-time job offer to rejoin Target following her graduation in spring 2017.

Udezue started as an in-training buyer for haircare products, then switched into different segments in the beauty category over the next four years. From her previous accounting career, she brought attention to the numbers. "One of the things that you develop as a tax accountant is looking at numbers to make sure they make sense. Now, I could eyeball the numbers to find patterns. Just being critical of the data that is sent over to our team is helpful. I learned in audit, you have to be able to trace everything. Sometimes, I get data from vendors and I question it." Her technical skills with numbers allowed her to go deeper than some of her colleagues.

Not surprisingly, Udezue relied on her psychology studies the most, pointing out, "Understanding the consumer's motivations is super important. The worst thing to do as a buyer is buying stuff you like. You have to understand what is motivating people and have that insight." When I pointed out that the National Center for Education Statistics listed psychology as the sixth most awarded undergraduate degree in the US, Udezue reflected, "I didn't know that psychology degrees could go into advertising, human resources, or communications. It might have been a really good path for me."

Another aspect that helped her is her cross-continental upbringing in the US and Nigeria. She said, "Living in different cultures and countries helped as well because I don't look at things in the same way. I lived in the States long enough to understand a more traditional US point of view, but also have exposure to other ways that other people think, so I can bring some of that extra perspective to our decisions. It's an advantage." Finally, she uses her influence to help the small businesses whose products are sold in Target's retail locations by advising them on their packaging to improve their appearance on the store shelves. She enjoys these collaborative discussions with small business owners on their products.

Throughout her journey, Udezue always kept her passion for marketing at the forefront. When she could not find marketing roles, she relied on her accounting skills to build a career. Then, she set a major intention in pursuing her MBA to facilitate a desired career pivot to realize her dream.

Udezue's Key Skills:

- Determination, which Udezue displayed in meeting the PwC recruiter at her alma mater's campus.
- Diligence, which Udezue demonstrated in pursuing the academic programs necessary for each career goal.
- Self-care, which Udezue prioritized to switch careers from the private to public sector in favor of a better lifestyle.

Udezue knew her future career as a marketer waited for her, but it was matter of time for the switch to happen. From Udezue's story, I take away not losing sight of your goals, patience, flexibility, and taking advantage of your strengths to pay the bills. The role for you will come, but you also must steer your path towards it.

Michelle Udezue

WHERE DID YOU WORK?

Brand marketing

Tax accounting

Social media

Tax law

Public accounting

Accounting

Sales

WHAT CAN YOU DO?

TECHNOLOGY

CHAPTER TWELVE

EJIEME EROMOSELE: FROM EXPERIENCE CONSULTANT TO CUSTOMER SUCCESS EXECUTIVE

———

Ejieme Eromosele spent most of her career in customer-oriented roles, going between customer experience and customer success. To those outside of the industry, customer success and customer experience seem like two variations of a customer service role, that you hear being referred to nowadays as everything from customer delight agent to customer concierge. In reality, customer success is proactive in nature, finding ways to bring a product's value to the customer, and customer experience is more interactive, where the product becomes part of the customer's daily workflows (Jacobs, 2020).

After graduating from New York University (NYU) in July 2005, Eromosele joined Accenture's Customer Strategy Group as a management consultant to resolve customer service challenges for their clients. She worked on projects, including the

New York City 311 Citizen Service Center, which sought to streamline residents' access to all the city's services through a "one-stop" service delivery model—it became a national standard. She also set up outsourced call centers in India and the Philippines for private sector customers. After four years, Eromosele pursued her MBA at NYU Stern School of Business, then returned to the world of management consulting, but this time, at PwC. She continued to strengthen her expertise in customer experience strategy and execution with global customers.

In October 2015, *The New York Times* published their new strategy called "A Path Forward," which outlined its plans to sustain its growth through a "user-first" mantra. In their words, they would "prioritize user experience and the needs of our customers over hitting quarterly revenue targets." Kate Harris, a director of product and Eromosele's MBA classmate, encouraged her to apply for a customer experience role, the first of its kind in the organization. In early 2016, Eromosele joined as a managing director in the consumer marketing department to help the one hundred sixty-year-old newspaper think about how to be a subscriber-first business.

Eromosele relied on her ten years of experience in management consulting by telling compelling analytical stories, selling stakeholders across teams to get their support, communicating with impact, and influencing without authority. Her first-year mission: secure corporate consensus around the vision for customer experience at *The New York Times*. Her scope of work was holistic, initially focused on "How do you shift from marketing to product," and "How do you think about individual subscribers and not only large advertisers?"

She spent hours in the newsroom, working alongside those teams to understand their daily activities.

Her data-driven approach meant she could make sure the newspaper could measure incremental improvements in customer experience. She would combine this data with recommendations for other teams to implement to make changes. This hand off became a point of frustration as she shared, "Some of the initiatives, I would own, but the majority of them, I did not. I would support other teams. I left consulting to do the work and to own the work, but here, I continued to operate in an internal consulting role."

Eromosele channeled her discomfort into a job hunt in fall 2017. She spoke with mentors, both internally within *The New York Times* and externally, who encouraged her to create her own role in a smaller organization where she could own more. She spent time distinguishing what she was capable of and what she enjoyed doing. In her own words, "I'm really great at talking to customers. I'm really great at understanding their business problems and articulating how I can help them and figuring out how we as a business can help them." She also reflected on firms that interested her. Thinking about "what type of organization I wanted to work [in]" and "what type of function I wanted to do" helped her narrow her search to roles in an early-stage technology company in New York City.

As part of her research, one of her informational calls was with a leader of the Customer Experience Professional Association, who upon hearing about her experiences in management consulting combined with the recent tour of duty learning subscription revenue models opened Eromosele's eyes to the nascent field of customer success. The term itself was completely new to her! She characterizes her revelation as, "I wanted to be in a smaller company, but that was also frightening because I had never done tech, never worked in customer success, and never worked in a super early-stage, small company." As a former management consultant, she felt empowered knowing she could be "dropped into ambiguity" in taking on a new role in a new industry.

Eromosele began her online research on the customer success function, set up keyword alerts on LinkedIn, and started applying to openings on LinkedIn. Through this methodology, she found a job posting on LinkedIn for a client services role at Snaps (now called Quiq) that matched what she read about customer success roles. The company stood out to her because their cutting-edge technology looked like an evolution of what she started with at Accenture on customer service; it was the future of customer experience. In her final breakfast interview with Snaps CEO Christian Brucculeri, he was straightforward with her: "I've never hired someone who has not done startups before." He proceeded to candidly tell her all the reasons why she could fail in the role, but he concluded with, "I still want to hire you." In retrospect, she appreciated his candor and his ability to set expectations with her early on.

"It's important to live life as if everything is rigged in your favor," Paul Hannam quoted the thirteenth-century poet Rumi in his 2016 TEDx Talk. He interpreted the statement as "a way to look at your life as a process of looking for, finding, and following the clues—because when you approach life that way, you naturally look for what's more positive and what's more serendipitous." Eromosele's career choices were happy accidents that took her into the fields of publishing and technology startups. From our conversations, I learned Eromosele not only needed to connect the dots for others, but sometimes, she needed others to connect the dots for her to see the application of her prior experiences into her next role. While roles were unfamiliar, she approached them with curiosity and as a result, found success.

Eromosele set an intention on her career shifts, but she recognized the importance of "being more open to new things and taking risks." She felt she experienced a bit of serendipity by choosing the customer service group at Accenture early on in her career, then finding the next phases of the customer experience work in her subsequent roles.

Eromosele's Key Skills:

- Coaching (receiving and giving), which Eromosele received, guided her to customer success roles, and translates to her current team.
- Consensus-based decision-making, which Eromosele practiced at *The New York Times* to move the strategy forward.
- Influence without authority, which Eromosele learned through consulting with private and public sector organizations at Accenture.

She cultivated her customer experience knowledge in a variety of environments that when brought together, put her in a successful position in a new industry.

Ejieme Eromosele

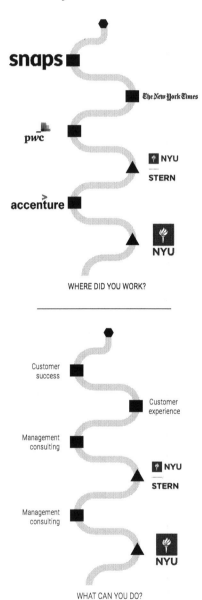

snaps

The New York Times

pwc

NYU
STERN

accenture

NYU

WHERE DID YOU WORK?

Customer success

Customer experience

Management consulting

NYU
STERN

Management consulting

NYU

WHAT CAN YOU DO?

CHAPTER THIRTEEN

ANA MARIA GOMEZ LOPEZ: FROM FINANCIAL SERVICES CONSULTANT TO FINANCIAL TECHNOLOGY EXECUTIVE

Ana Maria Gomez Lopez and I both arrived wide eyed to Cambridge, MA, in June 2016 to complete the Sloan Fellows MBA program at MIT Sloan. We shared an enthusiasm to maximize every hour of each day by immersing ourselves in the school's resources, ranging from academics to student life to startups. While our academic interests diverged, we repeatedly crossed paths in student life, such as in the Sloan Senate and the Graduate Student Leadership Institute, and in activities organized in our friend circle, including a bike ride across Martha's Vineyard or a Coldplay concert at Gillette Stadium. Gomez Lopez was extremely bright—an achiever, she finished college at twenty years old; hard-fought career transitions and a willingness to learn fueled her determination to succeed.

As Gomez Lopez approached her college graduation in spring 2003, she shared her job search with her economics professors. One of her professors offered her an entry-level role on his team in the pensions department at Telecom Colombia, the national telecommunications company headquartered in Bogotá. Gomez Lopez quickly found the manual work of verifying up to two thousand employees' eligibility for retirement pensions as monotonous and repetitive, so she taught herself a technical solution within Microsoft Excel, devised an automated system, and processed the information in larger batches. She explained her frame of mind: "How can I do this better; how can I do this faster; how can I do this to avoid manual mistakes?" That last point was important because one mistake could cause a miscalculation of a retired employee's monthly pension payment, likely their only cash in hand, and could result in extreme heartache for both the individual and her colleagues.

With the free time Gomez Lopez carved out of her day, her manager invited her to meetings about the pension's portfolio, where she not only saw familiar economic concepts, but also gained exposure to new financial ones. In these meetings, Gomez Lopez realized the pension's management fee seemed high, so she benchmarked the fees against other providers and compiled her findings for her manager, who negotiated a fee reduction and saved millions on behalf of Telecom Colombia.

Gomez Lopez deepened her financial knowledge by pursuing a part-time master's in finance in 2005. Through her classwork, she met Andrea, who worked for a dedicated pension fund called Protección, but in a commercial role selling its products to consumers and companies. Gomez Lopez was not aware of this type of retirement product growing up, but she knew could learn about it on her own, so she asked Andrea to submit her resume for an open role in 2006. She recalled the situation, admitting, "I don't like to speak without knowing what I'm talking about, so I had to study the variables that affect portfolios." Gomez Lopez excelled in the role as a wealth management advisor, selling retirement plans to clients outside of her network and educating them on the investment options. She went so far as to apply the modern portfolio theory from her classes to the investment decisions to be upfront with risk tolerance to her customers. She recognized her empathetic ability to "see through the lens of one person, then try to translate it, so the other person can have the same understanding."

Gomez Lopez and her husband, Carlos, relocated from Bogotá to Washington, DC, so he could complete his MBA at the University of Maryland. She passed the time taking English language classes to improve her speaking capability. In February 2008, she attended a political rally with other Colombians. She struck up a conversation with her neighbor in the crowd, Julián Hoyos Salcedo, who turned out to be the president of the Colombian-American chamber of commerce of Washington, DC, Virginia, and Maryland. Hoyos Salcedo saw potential in Gomez Lopez and hired her to organize the chamber's trade events between American and Colombian companies. She remembered this period fondly, saying, "It was the best time in my entire life." This positive sentiment triggered memories of attending many high-profile political events to drive Latinx voter engagement for the 2008 US presidential election.

The couple returned to Bogotá in fall 2009 and Gomez Lopez began an earnest job search by messaging her friends on Facebook, then meeting them for coffee a few times per week. Her friend, Catalina, shared Gomez Lopez's resume with a senior manager at EY, a management consulting firm. Concurrently, another friend, Diana, spotted an opportunity in a medical journal for a small healthcare company called AudioComIPS hiring an executive with finance expertise. She referred Gomez Lopez to interview with the CEO, who was in search of a college-educated, bilingual professional. Gomez Lopez interviewed and took a chief operations officer role at AudioComIPS in February 2010, with responsibility for the twenty-five branches around the country. She cut her teeth on business operations, including finance, human resources, and procurement: "I have never been in a small company. I have never managed human resources. Now, I was supervising the administrative areas. I'm disciplined—if I don't know something, I will reach out to my network to find out how to deal with the challenge."

Less than six months into this new job, EY approached Gomez Lopez for a role that required bilingual proficiency, business operations experience, and finance expertise on a newly formed team to support a banking client. While she met the criteria with ease, and her manager shared later that she "embodied the spirit of consulting with a work hard, play hard approach," Gomez Lopez's offer was for a position that was not commensurate with her pedigree. She left Audio-ComIPS, exchanging a lower salary for the career growth opportunity in a multinational company in summer 2010.

Gomez Lopez landed in the deep end of management consulting at EY. She had to familiarize herself with a new vocabulary, strategic frameworks, and how to create presentations for a customer's management team. When she saw her shortcomings, she took action. Gomez Lopez said of the role, "To really connect with my peers, I used to ask them: how do you do this and that, then they would share deliverables from other client projects for me to review. I had to make time to study these documents on my own after a long workday."

Gomez Lopez became acclimated to the rhythm of changing clients, projects, and roles in her first few years, while she "developed the muscles of the consulting techniques of how to present, make a diagnosis of an issue, bring that diagnosis to the C-level executives, and execute solutions to make the strategy tangible."

At the same time, Gomez Lopez started to prepare for the MBA admissions process, a goal she set for herself during her US stay. Her annual visits to the US expanded to include MBA campus tours. She applied to a couple of executive MBA degree programs and enrolled at MIT Sloan. Surrounded by classmates from thirty-four countries that provided a global view into business problems immediately excited her. She explored technology through the lens of financial services and social inclusion. Gomez Lopez shared that one of the main reasons she pursued a US-based MBA program was "to come back and to make a life in the US." However, the aftermath of the 2016 US presidential election in our fall semester made it increasingly difficult for her to realize the American dream. Employers either refused to sponsor an employment visa or complained about her level of bilingual proficiency.

Disheartened, but not defeated, Gomez Lopez returned to Bogotá in fall 2017, swiftly arranging meetings with her professional contacts about her blockchain studies at MIT Sloan. Laura Tovar, a classmate of ours, passed on a managing director role at a newly formed joint venture called the Digital Innovation Lab for Gomez Lopez's consideration. It was created by Porvenir, S.A., the competitor to Gomez Lopez's earlier employer Protección, and a local technology company. One of her interviews was with an executive who was the main stakeholder of her last client project at EY. He remembered Gomez Lopez's studious behavior and approved hiring her.

Gomez Lopez found gratification in the "real life" aspect of the Digital Innovation Lab. For her, this position brought together her finance expertise and her freshly developed startup mindset to lead a team incubating minimum viable financial products with social impact. If successful, these products would be commercialized for the local market. At one point, she requested that EY pitch for a consulting project opportunity at the Digital Innovation Lab. On behalf of EY, her former manager delivered the presentation. Seeing Gomez Lopez in a new light on the other side of the table, her former manager tried to hire her back. She declined. He reached out again six months later in fall 2018—the same week the joint venture collapsed—so she took him up on his offer to rejoin EY as a boomerang employee. The benefits of rehiring former employees are they may have improved thanks to the experiences they had during their time away and will bring back fresh knowledge, skills, and maturity (Arnold, 2021).

Gomez Lopez's second tour of duty at EY came with increased managerial responsibilities, exposure to senior leaders of the firm, and a sharpening of her existing skill set. The update to her LinkedIn profile's Experience section also brought messages from executive headhunters searching for talent for other management consulting and technology firms. One of these employers was Technisys, an Argentinian technology company expanding its operations to Colombia, seeking an executive to be responsible for the operations within the country, specifically the post-sales customer engagement process. The company caught Gomez Lopez's attention because their social mission to use technology to make financial services better resonated with her.

Gomez Lopez jumped at the chance to work at a company with social impact again, but the learning curve for her was steep, especially in the first six months. She called on a handful of her engineer friends to explain technical jargon used by her colleagues to illustrate customer issues. She also relied on her change management frameworks to call out persistent issues in the workplace. Finally, Gomez Lopez leveraged her empathetic ability to repair broken client relationships. A year in at Technisys, she has found her balance.

Gomez Lopez's largest success became her ability to leverage her ecosystem to find her next role. Her interest encouraged her to take on any challenge, especially knowing she could study it to increase her knowledge.

Gomez Lopez's Key Skills:

- Continuous learning, which Gomez Lopez relied upon to familiarize herself with new responsibilities and projects.
- Endurance, which fueled Gomez Lopez to push past setbacks and launch into new careers.
- Sociable, which enabled Gomez Lopez to acclimate in new environments and find new jobs.

While I had no doubt Gomez Lopez was an achiever, I learned of her flexibility in her story. Her story reminds us that sometimes our circumstances change out of our control. In these situations, we must stay focused on our career goals, lean on our networks, and be willing to learn new skills to move forward.

Ana Maria Gomez Lopez

WHERE DID YOU WORK?

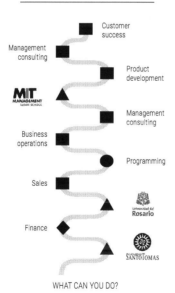

WHAT CAN YOU DO?

CHAPTER FOURTEEN

JONATHAN GODBOUT: FROM GOVERNMENT CONSULTANT TO SOCIAL IMPACT EXECUTIVE

When I learned about the field of social entrepreneurship in early 2013, I wanted to immerse myself in its ecosystem to not only learn from the risk-taking social entrepreneurs tackling problems in their local communities, but also to share my professional expertise with their impactful organizations in any way I could. The two premier social entrepreneurial institutions in this field were Ashoka and Echoing Green. That same year, I pursued a full-time role with the former and a volunteer role with the latter, and by the spring 2014, I became a member of Echoing Green's now-defunct Social Investment Council. A group of young professionals from across the US, mainly from the private sector, contributed to Echoing Green's capacity as advisors to its social entrepreneurial network. In the meetings of the local Washington, DC, chapter of the Social Investment Council, I met Jonathan Godbout.

Godbout was a senior managing consultant with IBM, with a side business in property development. Soon after his spring 2008 graduation from Colby College, he joined IBM in Washington, DC. Like many DC-based management consultants, he worked on government projects. For his first few years, Godbout's client was the US Department of Defense (DOD) Task Force for Business and Stability Operations in Afghanistan, which focused on bringing in foreign direct investment. Godbout proclaimed this work was "super interesting and exciting" as he learned about the soft power theory of economic stabilization to create jobs as a counterterrorism strategy. It built on his college studies of international economics, where he now had direct exposure to the mechanics of how these tools were applied to improve lives in devastated regions. Then, his next few years at IBM switched to cost-cutting efforts at DOD. The palpable excitement in his voice turned sour as he described this new project as "monotonous and soul crushing." He and the team prepared several in-depth analyses for budget efficiencies, but they were rarely actionable or enacted due to political pressures. Other process improvement projects came along, but they were never as interesting as his earlier work.

Godbout set a goal to find an interesting startup organization where he could make a difference while he built financial security in his day-to-day management consulting work. In the meantime, he sought refuge in IBM's pro bono consulting program. He continued to bill the minimum forty-five hours to meet his team's weekly utilization targets, while leveraging his extra capacity to work an additional thirty-five hours on social good projects that benefited from IBM's expertise and tools. He invited other consultants to join him in these volunteer endeavors.

At the same time Godbout spun up pro bono projects for IBM with organizations like Ashoka, he shared his boredom at work with a new acquaintance. "Through a mutual friend at a party, I met Dave, who was telling me about his experience at Echoing Green and the Social Investment Council. When I told him how much I missed the exciting project work with the DOD in Iraq and Afghanistan, he invited me to get involved. That's where things took off."

Godbout joined the Social Investment Council to help their social entrepreneurs in his personal capacity in 2013. He found a sweet spot of balancing his passion and lifestyle to help nonprofit organizations by completely immersing himself in the social entrepreneurship ecosystem. In early 2014 through Echoing Green, he advised the leadership of Freedom for Immigrants, a nonprofit monitoring human rights abuses faced by immigrants in detention. His involvement led them to invite him to serve on their board of directors, a role that he still holds seven years later.

Godbout and I met multiple times at the "brain trust" dinners organized by Echoing Green, where we would meet with a fellow to provide advice on a pressing business issue. He approached me about expanding the IBM pro bono relationship with Ashoka. He wanted to "replicate what we were doing with the Echoing Green Fellows with Ashoka Fellows through IBM." Given my purview of the organization in my role as director of talent operations, I recommended he connect with Nancy Welsh, who at the time was the executive director of Youth Venture, Inc. Welsh was new to the organization and had fresh ideas about the Ashoka subsidiary that she was responsible for; she and Godbout clicked right away. She actually saw an opportunity for Godbout and IBM to help her own nonprofit, Builders of Hope, scale its operations from the US to Africa.

Remember Godbout's side business? He developed a property construction and rehabilitation business in Cincinnati, Ohio. It stemmed from his passion for building construction, where he said, "I worked in my dad's plumbing business in Maine from ages twelve to twenty-two, so anytime that I could get back to construction, it felt familiar and enjoyable." So, when he learned about Builders of Hope's mission to construct houses for the less fortunate and the goal to bring the program to Africa, he was all in. He explained to me, "In the Northern hemisphere, we create affordable housing by building a lot of houses at once. But in the Southern hemisphere, the housing need is so great. While the relative cost of construction far exceeds the median income, you can't use massive scale to bring the costs down. In a place like Nigeria or Kenya, constructing five thousand homes at once won't get you an affordable home for the median household income. Even if we build houses at scale, it is not affordable to lower income populations. Instead of building houses all at once, they build their houses over time—foundation this year, walls next year, maybe a roof in three years. You need to think about housing in a different way."

Godbout found synergy with the vision for Builders for Hope, so he initially volunteered his time to help with fundraising for six months. He crafted a winning pitch to the just opened

MasterCard Labs for Financial Inclusion in Nairobi, Kenya. Secured by that initial capital raise for a six-month runway, he left IBM to join the nonprofit full time in fall 2015. Godbout remembered, "If an organization has enough funding to give me six months, I can figure something out on my own. I was going to some pretty remote places in Nigeria and Zambia trying to figure out, 'How do locals find work, how do you build a house, and how do you find an architect?' It was very different from being a management consultant, but in some ways, the same. The resources were different, but my approach was similar to an in-depth assessment for my public or private sector clients.

"The Builders of Hope team didn't have technologists, so they didn't have an idea of software to solve the problem. For me, it was just kind of exciting to dive into that." Within two years and many frequent flights between the US and different African countries, the Builders of Hope team developed and spun off a mobile application called iBUILD to connect laborers and homeowners for small-scale construction projects. The transparent marketplace unified the housing construction process in one place, democratizing access to affordable housing in regions affected by housing shortages.

Godbout became a cofounder and chief innovation officer for iBUILD, scaling the business to more than twenty employees in over four-and-a-half years. He managed the whole product development team. "I got really into the technology and I became a product manager. It was a big change. I applied project management frameworks to a startup environment. For the user interface design work, I applied what I learned designing presentations and approaching process improvement projects for my former clients."

During the COVID-19 pandemic, Godbout was unable to travel to Africa, so he shifted his focus back to an advisory role with iBUILD from Waterville, Maine, where his wife, Veronica, took a teaching position at his alma mater, Colby College. At the time of our conversation in early 2021, his former IBM colleague, Emily King, approached him to be the chief operating officer at Prospector, an early-stage startup to help investors fund mining projects using artificial intelligence and analytics. What attracted Godbout to this new opportunity was King's "promise to put jobs in central Maine. If I can create five to ten jobs in a small college town in Maine, it's going to help the community." Also, given his proximity to campus, he sought ways to bring technical and machine learning projects to the students, finding opportunities for a dozen student internships with social impact organizations from his network in the past year.

Godbout's determination to work for an organization with social impact is admirable. In his own words, "when you're in the corporate job, you don't often realize how your skills can be applied to social entrepreneurship, but there are many ways you can apply skills you learn working with Fortune 500 companies or governments to pursue passions in other sectors. You just need to get exposed to more people.

"Leadership in the twenty-first century is defined and evidenced by: what is the diversity measure of your personal and professional stakeholder network? This question is about your capacity to develop relationships with people that are very different than you. Despite the differences, they connect with you and trust you enough to cooperate with you in achieving a shared goal." These are findings shared by Roselinde Torres in her 2013 TED talk. She took a year of her career to study effective and ineffective leadership practices around the world. Godbout demonstrated this type of leadership as he broadened his professional networking by joining the Social Investment Council, Freedom for Immigrants, Builders for Hope, and ultimately, creating iBUILD. He invested time in developing relationships with each organization to fulfill his desire for a career with social impact.

Godbout's Key Skills:

- Collaboration, which Godbout leveraged to build volunteer teams at IBM, then displayed as he worked with the cross-continental teams for Builders of Hope and iBUILD.
- Communicating to executives, which Godbout practiced at IBM and with Echoing Green Fellows, then used to secure resources for the housing projects.
- Project management, which Godbout learned at IBM in corporate and pro bono work, then introduced in subsequent roles to keep initiatives on track.

Godbout laid a solid foundation to his career pivot by learning these transferable skills during his seven years at IBM and setting up his property development company. He set a goal and he achieved it. I would say his story is also one of patience as he sought an alignment of an opportunity, timing, and his skills before making the leap.

Jonathan Godbout

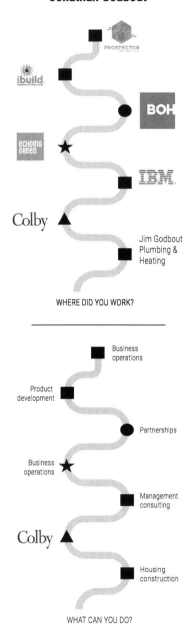

WHERE DID YOU WORK?

Business operations

Product development

Partnerships

Business operations

Management consulting

Colby

Housing construction

WHAT CAN YOU DO?

PART II

SKILLS
TO ADVANCE
YOUR CAREER

CHAPTER FIFTEEN

PERSONAL BRAND

———

"I am one of those jacks of all trades, who have done so many things."

This is how Sarah Harel described herself. She worked in the private and nonprofit sectors. We met in fall 2011, when her then roommate referred her to Civic, and she was assigned to help me with the project management for our client, NBC News. I welcomed her calm demeanor, self-direction, and organizational horsepower in the eighteen-hour days leading up to the Education Nation Summit at the iconic Rockefeller Center. Though our time working together was brief, Harel and I stayed in touch through different career changes.

During her job searches, I would challenge Harel by asking, "What have you done in this last role? How can you translate all of your different experiences into something that makes a little bit more sense for potential employers?"

Harel pointed out she thought my ability to help coach people "to the point of being specific with the job that they want" is an important part of the job search process and one she connected with. She took the advice to heart, bouncing ideas off an executive coach and mentors, until she realized a chief of staff role would suit her personality and skills. Since I held a similar role previously, I validated her findings to assure her she was on the right career path.

Harel showcased her abilities aligned to a chief of staff role and responsibilities by "distilling the functional skills into a summary and bullet points at the top of the resume, then talking about them in informational interviews."

She leaned into project management because she knew that could take her in many different directions career wise. Her choice to use a common business term of "project management" to describe her natural gift guided future employers to quickly understand how they could utilize her capabilities.

Harel became savvy at building relationships (both externally and internally) to get things done, which she picked up in an early career role as an executive assistant to a real estate developer. She shared, "Seeing what a CEO does at a 30,000-foot macro view was helpful and gave me the idea to look at things from the top to figure out who is interconnected." She also said she "found a sweet spot in being the voice in the room that can identify the people impacts of organizational changes," an attribute that was solidified when she stepped into a HR position with her prior employer, Understood.org.

Harel did not realize it at the time, but she had narrowed in on her personal brand.

ESTABLISH YOUR REPUTATION

"Credibility is, in a way, a higher bar than success. It means others look at you as a reliable resource and decision maker. It allows those who rely on you to know they can count on you, trust you, do business with you, and align with you," wrote leadership expert Lolly Daskal in an *Inc.* June 2017 article.

Before you can get digital tools to work for you properly, you need to show you have established your reputation in your career, field, industry, or sector. This reputation serves as your calling card. It shows you have the experience and credibility to help others. It shows you as a leader in your field. This is important, especially if you want to grow your business or switch careers.

Your personal brand changes over time and you can rebrand. It can be shared in a number of ways with others, including as an elevator pitch (both online and in person), through business networking events, or represented in your digital presence. You can also leverage LinkedIn as your digital portfolio to help you to rebrand when you are ready to make that move.

CREATING YOUR ELEVATOR PITCH

One of the most important pieces of your personal brand is your elevator pitch. The elevator pitch should be thirty seconds, which is enough time to relay information about yourself. It needs to be memorable and specific. You want to be able to share:

- Who you are;
- What you want to do;
- Answer the question, "How I can help you?"

Here are two examples:

Job Search Example: "Hi! I'm Asha; I'm a vice president at a tech company based in NYC and I'm looking for a similar role in Washington, DC. Do you know anyone hiring for senior executive operations roles in DC?"

When I read this example out loud, it was ten seconds. So, you can see thirty seconds is a long time to relay information. In the example, I share my name, what I am doing, where I am, and where I want to go, and ask if they know someone (not a company, but a particular person that is hiring for this type of role). For me, it was more important to highlight that personal relationship in my ask, rather than a specific company ask, because this type of role is not always advertised.

Business Development Example: "Hi! I'm Asha; I work at a tech company that helps enterprise companies to unify their customer experience management. What are the brands that stand out to you on social media?"

In this second example, I focused on business development opportunities versus looking for a new job. It runs shy of ten seconds. In this example, I highlighted my employer's work with bigger companies on "customer experience management." And because that term might not be familiar to you, especially if you work in a different industry or sector, I position the second statement as a question to allow you to weigh in and answer or ask more questions about why or how social media relates to customer experience management.

By having your elevator pitch formulated and ready to go, you will leave a positive impression on others. It can help you to open doors in a business networking event.

CARRYING A BUSINESS CARD

A strong element of developing your personal brand in the physical world is your business card. Some people joke that business cards are no longer needed in today's digital world, but they are important because they serve as a token or memory of an event—where you went, who you met, and additional context on a conversation for both you and the other person.

"An overwhelming 72 percent of people form an opinion about a company based on the quality of its business card," quoted Alice Jackson in a Design Hill February 2019 blog post as she pointed out that a business card design speaks favorably for a business.

Karen Preston-Loeb highlighted in a Furia Rubel Communications June 2017 blog post that "multiple business cards can be handed out in seconds at a networking event [without interruption to the conversation] versus entering data [into a personal device]." She goes so far as to mention, "While the majority of our population does have a personal electronic device, some prefer not to rely on theirs," with a reminder there are incompatible mobile applications or low to no battery devices in someone's hands. Analog is a good back-up to digital.

In the introduction, I shared how Reid Hoffman and Ben Casnocha describe how we are unfinished products. Remember to consider yourself as the product and the business card is what you leave with others that you interact with. Preston-Loeb simply described this as "image is everything," where the business card on hand shows proper planning and an appearance of professionalism. The business card is a professional representation of you.

For those of you doubting the relevance of a business card in today's increasingly virtual world, the *Forbes* Agency Council posted a wide range of opinions on the topic in November 2017. Ranging from immediately sending an email, connecting on social media to reasons like those listed above, the overwhelming sentiment was that business cards serve a purpose.

For more than ten years, I carried a personal card. My professional experience in the government and nonprofit sector meant limited to zero funds for employer-provided business cards. Also, I found when I hand out a personal card, people are less likely to spam me when they see my personal email. On a personal or business card, I make sure to have:

- Name;
- Email;
- LinkedIn URL (make sure you customize it);
- Social media handles: Twitter, Instagram;
- Mobile phone (optional).

I listed my phone number on earlier versions of my business card but found only one person to cold call me over the years. In countries where social messaging tools are more popular, contacts will add you using your mobile phone number right away to continue the conversation from a business meeting.

SHARING YOUR BUSINESS CARD

You can leave the flip side blank, so when you hand it over, you can write down where you met, what you spoke about, or a follow-up item to remind the recipient of your interaction. I met someone who printed "We Met...," along with a few blank lines, on the back of his business card to purposefully remember to write a message to the recipient. When I exchange business cards, I jot down a couple of words to remind the other person about a resource we discussed or an organization I am involved with, so we have an action to follow up with each other. As I mentioned, I use a personal card that does not have my work information, so I can write down the name of my employer to remind them of a business opportunity, including a potential collaboration, serving as a reference for a project or trading best practices.

RECEIVING A BUSINESS CARD

When you receive a business card, you can also write down notes or a reminder on the back. I may write down the name or date of an event where I received the card or a brief reminder of a follow-up item, such as scheduling a meeting, facilitating an introduction, or making a recommendation related to the conversation at the event. While my goal is to follow up within twenty-four hours, this written reminder is a helpful visual cue because I may not be able to tackle adding this person on LinkedIn as a connection and taking care of that next step in our interaction until a few days later, especially if I am traveling to an event. This personal reminder technique also reinforces your credibility to the other person—they take a mental note on how serious you are when they see you writing down the next steps. Daskal also emphasized how trustworthiness and accountability bolster one's credibility.

USING TRANSFERABLE SKILLS FOR YOUR PERSONAL BRAND

From the time he finished his undergraduate degree at the Instituto Tecnológico de Buenos Aires (ITBA) in winter 2007, Pedro Podesta wore multiple hats at his father's construction and real estate business in Buenos Aires, Argentina. In fall 2015, a wave of optimism hit the country as a newly-elected president and political party came into power, with a promise to bring Argentina back onto the global stage. With this momentum, Podesta felt "it was a good idea for our company to have someone with foreign relationships," and decided to pursue his MBA in the US.

Stephen Sacca paired us in a study group on the first day of classes in summer 2016, where our near-daily conversations trended towards the "what's next?" after graduation; sometimes, they were practical and sometimes they were aspirational. I use "near daily" because our cohort's exploration of the MIT ecosystem, including over forty programs dedicated to student entrepreneurship, colored our collective future outlook.

"I found the power of entrepreneurship to be very seductive, so why not?" reflected Podesta as he heard a third of our classmates' birth startups on ideas they either came to school with or accelerated with peers onsite. Encouraged by this flutter of activity, he vetted his own idea named Pirca, a peer-to-peer ride-sharing startup for commuters living in the suburban communities outside of Buenos Aires, with Wassim Matar, Bruno Nogueira, and Scott Durbin. They lived in the same apartment complex, so their kids' playdates provided ample opportunity to brainstorm. When the school's largest entrepreneurship competition opened its first-round applications in fall 2016, Podesta asked for my help to produce the startup's pitch. Having listened to hundreds of startup pitches, I advised that speaking about his personal journey was just as important as his idea. An hour before the deadline, he submitted the application with an authentic narrative that explained how his first-hand experience bore Pirca.

As the school year progressed, it became clear for Podesta that following the MBA, he should gain business strategy and finance work experience in another company to "be a better professional to come back to work for [his] family company." We had more than a few conversations about how his experience in real estate could lend itself well to a private equity company interested in real estate. He remembered, "For me, it was very hard to see how my profile could be interesting to these private equity companies. I learned a lot from talking to you about how to sell myself, especially since I knew I was capable of completing the due diligence on a real estate investment based on my experiences in the industry."

The job search concepts were foreign to Podesta. He said, "From you and our classmates, I learned what to look for as far as roles, where to apply, how to make my LinkedIn look good, what to put on my resume and what not to put on my resume, and how to sell myself as a target." We joked about his former mugshot-style photograph on his LinkedIn profile, which he switched after I convinced him to use a candid photo of him giving a presentation. That candid photo shows his true personal brand and what he wants to be recognized for; it is still his profile picture today.

Podesta's self-driven initiative landed him interviews with private equity firms, management consulting practices, and multinational companies with corporate real estate practices. Since he carried dual passports, he expanded his search beyond Argentina to Europe. Naturally, our study group conversations shifted to reframing his elevator pitch, where he recalled me pushing him a bit and suggesting, "Yes, you are an engineer, but why don't you share your skills this way?"

For example, he needed to demonstrate the project management skills he learned on the construction sites were transferable upstream to facility location selection and lease negotiation. The typical interactions between the corporation and the local stakeholders were relationships he was familiar with, because once a project broke ground, his team inherited them. Most importantly, the roles required someone with experience handling construction delays and knowing how to communicate these delays diplomatically to the key stakeholders. Ultimately, Podesta secured an offer from Amazon's design and construction team in Luxembourg.

CONCLUSION

Your personal brand can be cultivated and reinvented as you embark on your career pivots. With each transferable skill you earn, you can add to the narrative, demonstrate your proficiency, and grow your professional network. Now, it is up to you to shape how others see you.

CHAPTER SIXTEEN

DIGITAL TOOLS

——

"This is where I am supposed to tell you how great I am, and where my professional passions lie lol...If you've read this far and I still have your attention...nice to meet you. I hope my 'interests' can help me network with people that can offer insights into opportunities I may not be aware of or have even considered to try."

This is how Simone Williams opened her LinkedIn profile's "about" section. She wanted "people to see the humor in what I wrote. The next opportunity I get I want to have fun doing what I'm doing."

Starting her career as a human resources generalist, Williams found more success as a sales compensation specialist, where she spent the last fifteen years in media, not for profit, pharmaceuticals, and technology. She preferred the dynamic nature of the work, expressing "sales compensation is one of those areas where you never approach a problem in the same way twice because a company's strategy always shifts."

Our paths crossed at Sprinklr, where we worked together to design and pay out my department's compensation plans.

Her invaluable perspective helped me to understand a facet of compensation that I was unfamiliar with, while our shared understanding of the processes ensured a smooth outcome for the company and the employees. Following her departure in winter 2019, we stayed in touch throughout her job search.

After previously working with career consultants, Williams rewrote her resume and LinkedIn profile in her own style, approaching it with the mentality of "this is an intro to me. It's not me telling the company to hire me. Instead, it is saying what I'm looking to do in my next opportunity. I am at the point in my career where my LinkedIn profile should attract the right people I'm looking to work for. Like every viewpoint, the ideals surrounding 'fun' varies from person to person. If you don't have enjoyment in the work you do AND the people you're around, find the courage to walk away and lean into something new when opportunity calls." She focused the content around the types of roles she wanted to attract, how she enjoyed working, and how she wanted to be developed by a future employer. Williams LinkedIn profile's headline simply states, "All about Sales Compensation."

It was raw, honest, and pure Williams. Her goal to personalize the headline and "about" section in a way that felt true to her worked. Recruiters messaged her with, "This made me laugh so much!" as they quoted words in her profile back to her. Williams reflected, "They know so many people feel the exact same way, but those people don't have as much fun putting it on LinkedIn because everyone tries to stay professional." Her friends labeled it as self-deprecating, but Williams felt her approach was a differentiator that showed her true personality.

Williams's LinkedIn profile focused on her skills attracts up to five messages per week from recruiters. In early 2020, a recruiter from Kantar, a media company, sent a LinkedIn connection request, followed by an email to her personal address stating, "After reviewing your profile, I feel like your background aligns with an opportunity. I was wondering if you had a few minutes to spare to connect with me on a call? You may not be looking, but it's always best practice to hear what's out there in the market. You never know—this could be the opportunity of a lifetime." While the message caught Williams's attention, it was subsequent interviews with a senior vice president and a chief revenue officer that demonstrated alignment in what the company needed and what Williams brought to the table. She joined Kantar as its director of sales compensation in fall 2020.

YOUR DIGITAL PRESENCE

Take a moment to search for yourself online. I bet the first or second search result that appears is your LinkedIn professional profile.

When I type "Asha Aravindakshan" into the Google search bar, it takes half a second for the results on the first page to appear in this order:

- my LinkedIn profile,
- my Twitter profile,
- various versions of my biography appearing on event websites for speaking engagements,
- my Instagram profile, and
- my Facebook profile.

My guess is your search results page looks similar to mine, but maybe the order of social media profiles is slightly different based on how often you post to them. The exciting part of this discovery is that you control the content on these social media profiles and, in turn, on search results with your name. Not seeing results from platforms you control? Change it, by making the social channel work for you.

LINKEDIN

Years ago, I met a professor from American University, who declared, "Every student should be required to have a LinkedIn profile to graduate." I asked Shawn VanDerziel of the National Association of Colleges and Employers for his thoughts on this statement: "Absolutely, if you want to be found, you need to have a LinkedIn profile." He reiterated, "It's also a verification process. Most employers are going to complete an online search for you before you start a job to see if what you're putting out there to the world matches what you're giving them. At a minimum having that LinkedIn profile helps to verify that you are who you say you are because you are putting it out there publicly as well as you are sending it to me privately through your resume." Also, as a hiring manager or recruiter for any employer, you should also have a robust and fully filled-out LinkedIn profile for credibility.

As a hiring manager, I always check a candidate's LinkedIn profile to make sure the details align with their resume. Six years ago, my manager invited a candidate to fly in for an interview (on their own dime). The candidate's resume showed they had stopped working earlier that year, but her

LinkedIn profile showed she started working in a new role at a financial services firm a month or two earlier. When I asked my manager about it, he was not aware the candidate had taken another job and was clearly confused about why she flew in for the day to meet with our team. During a panel interview, three of us and the candidate were seated around a table in my office, and I had her resume in front of me for reference. Twenty minutes into the discussion, I asked the candidate about her intention of leaving her new role to join our team. The candidate looked confused at my question, then proceeded to reach over to grab the resume in front of me to see how I knew she had a new job. Of course, it did not appear on the document; it was the version she used in her job application. I explained I saw the information posted on her LinkedIn profile. She turned red with embarrassment and withdrew her candidacy as she had no desire to leave her new company.

More recently, I interviewed a candidate who applied to several roles at the same time and started a new position before he secured an interview with Sprinklr. His resume showed he was still employed by his previous company, but his LinkedIn profile indicated he joined a new firm a few weeks prior to our conversation. When I asked him if he was serious about our role, he said he was still interested in the role because it aligned to his career goals.

Both stories are cautionary tales of how recruiters and hiring managers utilize the publicly available information you posted on social channels, such as LinkedIn, during a recruitment process. "Many recruiters contend that candidates are stretching the truth on their resumes [and LinkedIn profiles]," according to Monster's *The Future of Work* 2021 special report, while at the same time, "two-thirds of employers think candidates could do a better job articulating their skills more clearly."

Remember you are more than your job and more than your education. In Monster's employer survey, they found "globally, 59 percent of employers are primarily looking for a resume [or LinkedIn profile] to demonstrate a candidate's skills. Candidates, however, want to show their values more than their skills. Luckily, there is some agreement: candidates and employers both ranked skills and personality as the top two factors a resume [or LinkedIn profile] should demonstrate." By populating additional sections of your LinkedIn profile, you can have a well-rounded profile that shows the viewer who you are as a human being.

At the end of Part II, you will find a bonus chapter entitled "Guide to Your LinkedIn Profile" with more information about the important sections of a LinkedIn profile and how to set it up to be found in recruiter searches.

BOLSTERING YOUR RESUME

Vijay Swamy started to explore opportunities in Silicon Valley for jobs at the intersection of retail and technology in fall 2019. Once his search became more active, a technology recruiter gave him this advice: "You need to have your resume reviewed as it will go through an applicant tracking system (ATS) that applies standardized filtering, based on the keywords in the job description." An ATS is a recruiting software used by companies to manage their job descriptions, open positions, and job candidates. The last time Swamy had his resume reviewed was informally by me during our business school days.

To further illustrate the point, Swamy described the funnel of job applications into a company. "The job description is posted on multiple different sites, such as your company's website, LinkedIn, and Indeed. All of the resumes submitted to these sites are funneled through the same ATS, owned by the company. In order to keep moving through this funnel to reach the recruiter, it's extremely advantageous that you check all of the boxes in terms of matching the job description. That's the only way to stand out from the sheer volume of applicants."

With his focus on the top of the funnel, Swamy learned about Jobscan, a website that helps job seekers optimize their resumes for keywords. He uploaded his resume on the first screen, and next, he copied and pasted the text of his dream job's description on the second screen. The portal analyzed the two inputs and showed the keyword match results on a third screen. There was only a 30 percent text match, which shocked him. He recalls, "Surprisingly, I knew this was the perfect job for me. This is the exact kind of role where someone would love to hire me for it, yet they wouldn't see my resume or they couldn't talk to me because the ATS filtered me out."

I had a similar eye-opening experience in my first attempt using Jobscan. I found a job with the dual title of "VP / Chief of Staff," both of which are roles that I held. When I went through the steps with Jobscan, it showed only a 50 percent title match. I was stumped. As I dug into their analysis, it correctly showed that the term "VP," albeit an abbreviation for vice president, did not appear in any form on my resume. My inference that my current title, written out as vice president, was good enough for the keyword match to VP was wrong. Upon listening to my story, Swamy confirmed it with his own, then said, "When the ATS is scanning for the exact job title and the job title is not on your resume, it might deem you as not a good fit for the role." Lesson learned!

Swamy took the feedback provided by Jobscan to heart and adjusted his job search strategy, "I'll look at a job description to see if it fits me, then feed it into Jobscan to see the differences between the job description and my resume. I would then refine my resume based on the analysis. I ended up spending an hour per job application for customizing my resume." He further qualified the last statement with, "I only applied for a limited number of jobs that made good sense for me, which resulted in me having a really good success rate for interviews—close to 50 percent."

For those of you looking at the one-hour figure wondering how you will prioritize the time, Swamy shared, "This process helps you to look at your resume and job description on a deeper level. Most importantly, it helps you downstream. When you interview for the role, you learn to play up the traits that you possess and the hiring manager listed, then play down the others. I became more thoughtful in how I presented myself and how I approached interviews."

Still not convinced? Swamy recommended, "Save the custom version of your resume that you submit and the job description together, so you can go back to review them during the interview process. It becomes a cheat sheet because you already highlighted it and made notes. You now have a good idea of what your talking points should be when you're being interviewed." The upfront time investment helps you continuously during the job search process.

As we concluded our discussion on his experiences, Swamy cautioned, "With any of these tools, they are there to help you to overcome some of these filtering mechanisms, but they are not 100 percent reliable. In other words, even if they help you get through the filtering, you have to face a recruiter, who will determine your qualifications. So go find the jobs, find the positions that you are confident matches your skills, then, use the tools to get through the filtering mechanism."

PLACEMENT

Jose Siade hit the job market following a corporate restructuring at his previous employer in fall 2020. As we saw in the year's major headlines, the COVID-19 pandemic devastated businesses, who downsized, restructured, or closed due to structural changes in the economy. He dusted off his resume and began applying for executive-level jobs. Within three to four months, he progressed through several rounds of interviews for product management roles with a few different firms; then all of it came to a screeching halt—all three firms notified him in the same week they chose to go with another candidate who was a better fit.

Instead of seeing defeat, Siade saw an opportunity to change his job search strategy: "I needed to rethink this strategy to get more opportunities—better opportunities. Let's see if a career coach can really help me to achieve that level." With humility, he explained, "Things change. Between my last two job searches in 2005 and 2017, I noticed some changes. Back then, I used similar job search strategies and resume format, but this time in 2020, I could see less progress. I could get through recruiting to the hiring manager, but when it came to the decision, I did not receive a job offer."

After searching for career coaches, Siade discovered Placement, a comprehensive solution that provided a technical platform, classes, blog, and career coaches. He immersed himself in their services, sharing his feedback with me. Placement's main product is their job search platform, which surfaces opportunities, organizes them in a Kanban board, and prompts you to enter the details of your interviews. The super-organized Siade described the tool as "great for someone who's not well-organized with their job search. It's drag and drop, so you can easily move job openings through the stages. It stores your edited resume and cover letter, together with the online job posting and recent news you researched, so you have it in one place. It will save you ten to fifteen minutes per application, compared to organizing everything offline." Given my own experience tracking over three hundred job applications in a spreadsheet in 2018, I welcome an online tool that can help keep you organized during the job hunt.

Siade candidly requested a career coach that understood technology and executive hiring. His specificity worked. Once introduced, they met every couple of weeks, reviewing a weekly task list to attend the Placement workshops, update his LinkedIn profile, prepare for interviews, and develop another version of his resume.

"The resume templates were great," continued Siade. However, the career coach advised him to trim his twenty years of professional experience into one and half pages by explaining, "You have five seconds to catch somebody's attention. When they see a two-to-three-page resume, they're not going to read it. Ideally, it's one page, but that may feel like you're cutting bone, so get it down to one page and a half and let's see how that works." Siade felt "the shortened length was getting most of my points across in my seniority and everything else. It was readable by the ATS and reflected that 'Hey, this is somebody that I want to hire.' This resume is a tool that will get me employed. I was ready to roll." He attributed this change in his attitude to his career coach's guidance.

He started to see an increase from 10–30 percent on securing interviews. He explained, "I took the two previous versions of my resume and adapted the best content to the Placement templates, so it might have been a combination of me picking better roles and the format, but I was seeing progress."

Siade also used Placement's cover letter templates to his advantage, based on a recommendation from his career coach. Once again, the coach advised, "Less than 10 percent of online applications require a cover letter. If you write a great cover letter, imagine the person on the other side reading it for two seconds. They see this candidate's interest, showing that you read the recent news, you read about the company, and you are relating your skills to the company. The cover letter can push a candidate over the line." A good cover letter takes less than an hour (and decreases over time as you get used to it) in his experience. Monster's *The Future of Work* employer survey points out, "In the US, only 11 percent of employers view cover letters as an effective resource." Be judicious with your time management, but invest time in differentiators to your application, especially if it is without a warm referral.

Siade was much less enthusiastic about the caliber of the opportunities presented to him by Placement. Of twenty potential roles, he was "excited about one, gave a thumbs up to seven, and a thumbs down to the rest." He felt "it was bringing up a lot of junior- to director-level roles. For a senior executive, like me, it was not going to bring a lot of value." His coach addressed it, by saying, "You may be too senior for the websites that Placement is referencing to present these jobs." The other aspect of Placement that Siade leveraged was their blog. He stated, "It's got everything that you need." I also found the blog posts to be thorough.

After the COVID-19 vaccination distribution expanded within the US and Congress passed the American Rescue Plan Act, businesses became optimistic for the economic rebound and started to advertise for new job openings in February 2021. Siade noticed an increasing volume of job postings, especially many more that listed "remote" in the location field. He found interesting roles through LinkedIn searches, business school alumni, and professional contacts.

A marketing solutions role at LPL Financial surfaced in a LinkedIn job search and he thought, "I'm a very good candidate for this role." After applying, he met fairly quickly with the hiring manager, then completed four more interviews before he found out he was not selected for the position in favor of a candidate with more marketing experience. However, in delivering the news, the hiring manager also shared some positive feedback: "I loved your profile, Jose. I think you would be amazing for this new product management role that I am opening up on my team."

Siade restarted the interview process with LPL Financial. After five more interviews, he received an offer for the role of senior vice president of digital products to start in May 2021. When asked about his success with Placement, he said, "Half of it is the tool and half of it is you actually using what the tool provides." Overall, Siade is positive about the experience: "It's a no brainer. If you're in this job search situation and you've got some years of experience or you're struggling because you haven't done a job search in the last year and a half, then definitely, give Placement a try."

CONCLUSION

A twenty-first century job search requires digital tools in addition to your resume. The three digital tools are representative of the key actions for your job hunt: create a digital portfolio (LinkedIn), get in front of recruiters (Jobscan) and organize your applications/interviews (Placement). As illustrated in this chapter, this tool set is complementary to your personal brand and business networking, serving as a platform to showcase your transferable skills to those you know and want to know.

CHAPTER SEVENTEEN

BUSINESS NETWORKING

"I was in a really happy time—I got married, then a month later, I got laid off."

This is how Elizabeth Villa described the months after the last time I saw her in spring 2019. She was responsible for events in Sprinklr's marketing department, where she grew the team and shaped its portfolio over five years, based on her previous ten years in marketing and event planning in the healthcare, beauty, and technology industries. When leadership outsourced her team's work, she felt crushed. "When you build something like that, you really feel like they can't live without you. But really, you're just replaceable."

I appreciated Villa's ability to produce quality events for business development. When I saw a few experiential marketing roles posted online, I asked if I could connect her to the job posters and she agreed. She reflected, "I'm not the type of person who really sits still. I never say no to anything." Since I leveraged my event planning skills at Civic, I hoped Villa would do the same at a marketing agency or in-house in the marketing department at a larger company.

The former vice president of experiential marketing at Vox Media, a media conglomerate, and a Chief member posted in our member portal her team needed a senior manager. Given we shared the commonality of both belonging to Chief, I felt comfortable reaching out to her. Within two days of my warm introduction, they connected over email, with Villa generously offering to refer others to open roles if she was not a fit. When she interviewed with another member of the experiential marketing team, Hall Carlough, both realized she was too senior for the role, but Villa asked to keep in touch for any contracting opportunities.

Villa moved forward with her job search. She met weekly with a career transition coach, who started their initial meeting with, "I just want you to be happy." They discussed aspects of the job search process and Villa received resume advice, recounting, "He was like, 'Here's what you need to highlight about yourself and how you need to talk about yourself,' so I thought that was really beneficial for me because I know the value that I can bring to the position, but I don't always sell myself very well."

Two weeks later, Carlough reached out about a contracting opportunity for a project for Lightlife Burgers to launch their plant-based burger with a food truck tour in summer 2019. They had less than six weeks to kick off the multicity, multi-country tour through the US and Canada. Villa's motto: "I never say I don't know how to do something because I'm a smart person and I'm not lying when I say, 'Okay, I'll figure it out.'" She accepted the consulting project and described, "It was like having a full-on adult internship because I learned so much about stuff that I didn't know that

I didn't know." Villa did figure out what they needed for a successful campaign and documented it in a playbook for the Vox Media team, who wrapped the tour after she took a full-time role with ADP, the online payroll company. She said, "Vox Media was a wonderful bridge between Sprinklr and ADP because I got to do something totally different. I got to feel useful, during a time when I wasn't sure whether I was going to get a job or not. It was awesome."

"Now, from a brand perspective, when I work with a marketing agency, I know what is happening on the other side. I know better questions to ask when it comes to working with agencies." From Villa's perspective, the Vox Media experiential marketing project provided her with a new understanding of that world, which will benefit her in her career as a corporate event planner.

Based on the title or job description, Villa could have dismissed the Vox Media opportunity I shared, but her open-mindedness allowed her to meet the marketing team for an informational interview and build new connections. Then, her flexibility in her employment (consultant versus a full-time role) allowed Vox Media to find a way they could bring her expertise to the team. The summer project was a win-win for both Villa and Vox Media.

BECOMING A FEARLESS NETWORKER

You have established your brand, created your elevator pitch, printed out business cards to take to events, and strengthened your LinkedIn profile.

You are now ready for networking, with these eight proven techniques. Business networking is one of the best ways to help grow your career and your professional networks.

PREPARING FOR AN EVENT

The best way to prepare for an event is with pre-event research, starting with the speaker(s). This works for both in-person and virtual events. You will want to check out their LinkedIn profile, company biography, and social media streams for a well-rounded perspective of them and their interests to create specific questions. This research will also help you find commonalities, which you can incorporate into your questions to ask during or after their session and make you memorable. This prep takes ten to fifteen minutes but is worth it. I aim to have this prep completed twenty-four hours or more before the event, so I do not run out of time to complete it—it is that important to me. I've had this practice for eight years and it always works, especially when I want to meet a speaker—and I always do!

Then, you will want to plan for your big moment by being prepared and proactive:

- Listing the target speaker(s) names, session times, rooms/meeting URL;
- Writing questions to ask during the session;
- Writing remarks/comments to say post session, likely one-on-one with the speaker;
- Setting aside business cards for your target speaker(s)—you do not want to run out of cards for your big moment! Also, you can prewrite a couple of reminders (mention

that you will follow up for a meeting or a coffee) on the back of the business card to save time in the exchange.

Sarah Harel shared, "Networking takes work... to build your network, to really dive in by putting yourself in these uncomfortable situations, and to broach conversations with people that you don't know at all." She vouches for my methodology and described her own pre-event research: "I have at least one person in mind that I am going to speak with at the event. Then, I make note of a couple of questions to start a conversation: how many of these events have you been to, how long have you been part of this network, etc."

When I prodded Harel to think of a standout moment, she chimed, "It's basically every time I go to an event." With some further prodding, she pointed to a spring 2019 career event, where the former senior vice president of people for The We Company spoke at a fireside chat. Harel stepped into an HR role a couple months before, so she was eager to ask about potential career paths. As the session winded down, Harel approached the executive, remembering, "It made a huge impact on me to have a conversation with a person that was very high level and get their take on my career."

More recently, Harel participated in virtual networking events for the media and entertainment industry, where she honed in on sessions where the presenters shared how they handled challenges in their career. While most people are quick to dismiss stories from others in different industries as they do not apply to their situation, I applaud Harel for her open-mindedness because of the transferable learning from the stories.

If you are invited to a professional networking event without a speaker, you can check if the organizer published the guest list online before the event, then research who will be in attendance. That way, you can focus your attention on finding those attendees at the event. As you can see, I am not a fan of walking into a room without a game plan. If the guest list is not available before the event, then at the event, you can introduce yourself, with your elevator pitch, to the organizer to see who they think you should meet. As part of hosting the event, these folks have a vested interest in making sure that you enjoy the event. Also, they are aware of who has already entered the room. Then, you can quickly look up any LinkedIn profiles to create your talking points before you approach other attendees at the event. This approach makes a professional networking event less daunting.

FINDING COMMONALITIES TO MAKE NETWORKING EASIER

Nicole Williams, formerly LinkedIn's in-house Career Expert, spoke with Meredith Vieira about her top tips for finding a job at any age. She highlighted, "It is not networking at a big event, but being out and about and being able to approach people." She recommended simple trips to "the coffee shop or dog park," where you can build some level of rapport and turn the conversation into something more meaningful. Williams recommended that in your first interaction, "You are not asking for a job, but asking about things you have in common with conversation starters," such as the beverage you are ordering or the type of dog you have. "It's a confidence builder to get out there."

As Williams described, this first interaction may happen when you least expect it. Sasi Yajamanyam found a new job during his daily bus commute. In 2009, Yajamanyam commuted by bus from his home in Falls Church, VA, to his office at the International Monetary Fund in Washington, DC, where he was a technology consultant. He read a book to pass the time. One fall day, the woman seated next to him asked about the book in his hands, *The Future of Management* by Gary Hamel. They started chatting about the book and over the next few months, became friends, trading book recommendations, and debating new ideas. Her name was Kavitha Venkita and she oversaw the technology research practice at CEB (now, Gartner).

Not only did they live in the same neighborhood and share a similar taste in books, they found another commonality: working in the same field. Even after Yajamanyam wrapped up his consulting gig and changed commutes, he stayed in touch with Venkita. In early 2011, he approached her about potential opportunities at CEB. It turned out she had an open role on her team, which he applied to and accepted. Eighteen months after they sparked a friendship on the bus, Yajamanyam joined Venkita's team, and they continued to ride the same bus to work every day.

SETTING UP INFORMATIONAL INTERVIEWS

Another method to cultivate relationships is informational interviews. When Patrick O'Brien started his job hunt in fall 2020, he aimed to have referrals submit his resume for job openings. His goal: "I'm not sending a resume in without talking to people." First, he narrowed in on a particular role in software companies, stating, "I figured out what I want to do on a day-to-day basis. It's called different things in different places, like solutions engineer, solutions consultant, or cloud architect. So, instead of focusing on the title, I checked the job description for keywords, like 'solutioning,' because to me, that's an indicator that you're going to be talking to customers and figuring out what the right combination of services and products is for their particular problem statement."

Then, O'Brien set aside thirty minutes each day "to review all of the job opportunities that I identified to be a good fit. Then, in a spreadsheet, I keep track of the whole life cycle and my action items from 'I just spotted it' to all the way through to an interview." O'Brien researched online job posts, identified a handful that met his criteria for a presales consultant role in software companies, then used LinkedIn to research first- or second-degree connections that held similar roles at his targeted companies. By sending a personalized LinkedIn message to request fifteen minutes of their time to discuss the company and their role, he secured their interest and held meetings with everyone he asked. Then in the conversations, he asked questions about the role and ultimately requested an employee referral. He recalled, "You got to get on the phone and show that you're human and you're likable. Most of the time, they will say, 'You should talk to my colleague,' which helps you to continue the conversations with the target company."

In this scenario, where the entire interaction may be virtual, you need to establish a rapport before asking for the referral. In the past, when I could not find a contact for my target company, I submitted my resume for a role, then asked a second- or third-degree connection for an informational interview about the company and their role. In my outreach, I let them know I already submitted my resume for the role, so they are aware I will not be pressuring them to submit mine in the call (and therefore, decline participating in the call). This tactic worked to learn more about the company. At the end of these calls, once they better understand my qualifications for the role, they may reach out to the recruiting team to recommend me for the role. The recruiting team is happy to tag an employee as a referral source in the system.

LEVERAGING VOLUNTEER OPPORTUNITIES

Harel found opportunities to expand her professional network and leadership skills outside of the workplace. She joined Ellevate Network, a professional group for women, as a member in 2015. She signed up for an Ellevate Squad, a twelve-week program, where a group of ten to twelve women met for thirty to sixty minutes and rotated on self-nominated topics weekly.

When it was her turn, the squad supported Harel's job search by asking, "What are you doing to expand your network?" Then, she spent time crawling through each person's LinkedIn connections to make a list of those contacts at firms she was interested in. In a subsequent squad meeting, she asked them for advice, "Do you know anyone that I can talk to?" These actions led to productive informational interviews with both private and nonprofit sector employers, growing her professional network. While each squad officially disbands after the twelve weeks, she keeps in regular touch with its members years later.

Now, after participating as a member in different squads for a few years, Harel became a volunteer leader for the squads, running them according to Ellevate principles. She built her muscle on facilitation skills, including "keeping track of everyone's backgrounds, then being able to pull in those people into the weekly discussion to impart their knowledge on the others."

BUILDING YOUR OWN COMMUNITY

After working six-and-a-half years in an architecture firm, O'Brien moved from Dallas, TX, to Austin, TX, in summer 2011. He wanted to explore his curiosity in online communities, which formed on social media, uniting those with shared interests. Once he recognized his passion for it, he "got involved with in-person meetups of community managers in Austin to learn more and thought, 'If I could replicate that experience online, then it could lead to good things.' Also, I started to meet a bunch of people in industries and companies that I would actually want to go work for."

O'Brien cultivated this interest by starting his own event series for community managers and posting them on Meetup. com, a free site to share your events with those outside of your own circle. He became the de facto coleader of the community managers for more than a year—an unpaid, volunteer role. Also, he followed hundreds of community managers on Twitter and more than four hundred followed him back. His exchange of ideas occurred in person and online. The community managers viewed him "as an expert. This guy really knows what he's talking about and is opening doors for others because he became an expert." Although O'Brien did not hold a full-time role in community management, he built credibility through the skills of volunteering, business networking, and event planning.

Following a year and a half of immersing himself into the community management scene, O'Brien presented his findings to local businesses, including the Dachis Group, a social enterprise consultancy. Their Fortune 500 clients sought ways to better manage and scale knowledge within their companies. To satisfy their needs, Dachis Group hired O'Brien as a business manager responsible for their Social Business Council, infusing his knowledge of online communities into the client business. He turned his passion into a full-time role.

"It pays to be unpaid. Giving back can increase your odds of getting a job. In fact, people without high school diplomas are 51 percent more likely to find employment if they pitch in their free time," wrote Rachel Sylvester in *Real Simple's* December 2020 issue.

BUILDING YOUR OWN COMMUNITY THROUGH A PODCAST

"How do you know when you found that next career?" was the weighted question posed to Sonali Batish by her teenage daughters. They were curious about their mother's next steps as she stepped away from a twelve-year career in the consulting business created with her husband, Ajay.

An engineer turned COO, her own experience demonstrated "our lives are already so exponentially non-linear." So, Batish sought "to build a community of women who experienced successful career transitions and create a platform that allows women to embrace their career transitions, one story at a time." This idea manifested into the *My 2.0* podcast she launched in fall 2020, taping thirty-two episodes in eight months, with over 1,500 downloads globally. She approached female executives in her network for the first ten episodes, who then referred other guests from the corporate, entrepreneurship, and military domains. "I have the ability to give a very concrete platform to someone to share their experience, which is immensely helpful to others." She spent five hours each week recording a conversation, editing it to a consumable twenty-five minutes, then advertising each episode to her social networks. Batish's diligence did not go unnoticed as she learned that *My 2.0* reached Feedspot's top five of "The Most Career Minded and Working Women Podcasts of 2021."

Batish's success with her podcast is leading her to launch a second one in fall 2021, focused on women executives who scaled technology companies. This new endeavor is linked to her aspiration to get more female founders to start, scale, and sell companies. She stated, "My goal is to experience share through women CEOs who have successfully scaled a business, so that we can de-risk and demystify scaling. In a couple of years, I want to be on this career path, so the more I am exposed to CEOs, COOs, and the types of companies who have done this, then the more information I'll have when I am ready." She not only determined her next steps, but also plotted her own course to understand what it takes once she reaches there.

PREPARING FOR VIRTUAL NETWORKING

For those of you looking for an online option for virtual networking, Al Tepper, founder of a marketing consultancy called TepFu, developed his own methodology on LinkedIn. He likened LinkedIn networking to attending a dinner party "where you would not blurt out what you do in your initial greeting." He recommended generating reciprocity through kindness by liking, commenting, and sharing another's posts. Those actions will turn into website notifications for the person whose posts you are interacting with. Tepper's engagement strategy is "5-4-3-2-1," where you spend 5 minutes 4 (for) 3 likes, 2 comments, and 1 share of another's content. Then (and only then), you can send a connection request with a personalized message to the person. Since you built rapport through your engagement strategy, this person should not be surprised and welcome the outreach. This approach can also work on other social channels, including Facebook, Instagram, and Twitter, where you have multiple ways to engage with content.

FINDING EVENT SPEAKERS

I use online outreach for organizing events. In fall 2020, I planned an event about the impact of social media on the 2020 US presidential elections for the MIT Sloan Club of New York, the local alumni chapter for the business school, where I serve on the board of directors. On Twitter, I read an article by Elizabeth Culliford, a Reuters journalist who specializes on the exact topic. I sent her a direct message through Twitter, pitching my event idea and asking her to take part. She agreed! A few weeks later, I read another article on Twitter about the NYU AdObserver project that aligned to this subject and sent a cold email to their mailbox, to which Laura Edelson responded to participate in the event. In her response, she flagged that she had a prior affiliation with MIT and she knew Culliford. I felt their familiarity with each other would work well in the webinar.

Finally, for an academic perspective, I emailed the MIT Sloan Office of External Relations for recommendations on lecturers to participate and they recommended Dean Eckles, who wrote a timely article on the issue. I cold emailed him about the event, with the Office of External Relations copied, and he also agreed to be part of it. The whole event came together as a webinar that winter, with only virtual introductions.

CONCLUSION

You have to be able to cultivate your professional network by adding to it. Discovering thought leaders and like-minded professionals through events is a powerful way to build your network's strength over time. You are now ready to go out into the world and make the most of events that you attend. This skill is right at your fingertips.

Notes:

_____

_____

_____

_____

_____

_____

CHAPTER EIGHTEEN

ADVICE TO EMPLOYERS

——

Finding the right talent for your organization can be daunting without a rich pipeline of potential recruits steeped in the same values as your own. The solution is right in front of you in your university's students and alumni worldwide. For example, my GW community has shared values of civility, integrity, and service, while my MIT community exudes mind and heart. One way to understand this is to think about when you run into someone from your hometown—that familiarity or knowing feeling is what I mean. So, when you approach another alumni or student from a school you attended, the interaction immediately connects you back to your shared values.

I navigated the roles of job hunter and employer throughout my career by leaning on the career services programming that both my alma maters offer to both students and alumni.

While completing my undergraduate degree at GW, I took advantage of the Center for Career Services (the Center) from my first semester. I would pick up their annual guidebook to read the latest resume tips, then each semester, I used the free resume review service to obtain feedback on any new language that I added after each internship was completed. It was immensely helpful to have a second set of eyes from the career counselors and to incorporate their changes to make my resume even stronger. Also, I participated in on-campus recruiting with at least two companies.

As an alumna, I attended GW career fairs to understand the available roles, take a new headshot in the photo booth, and to practice my elevator pitch with the recruiters in attendance. I also attended these career fairs as an employer to meet potential hires. At the GW career fair in spring 2014, I met Jordan Gross, then a junior. She lined up a summer internship with Macy's and planned ahead for the fall semester by checking out the employers at the career fair. That afternoon, she was the only one student I met that was thinking ahead. We chatted about our experiences in the School of Business. Gross was sharp and personable. She left her resume with me. A few months later, when I was ready to hire fall interns, I reached out to Gross to join my talent operations team at Ashoka, and she accepted.

Now, in my current role, I post any job openings from our recruiting platform to my LinkedIn and Twitter profiles to share them widely. The recruiting platform generates customized employee referral links in social posts, so any person that uses them is tagged as my referral, which is visible to the recruiters and as such, may result in a higher likelihood of an interview for the role. In nine months, seventy people applied for jobs as a result of my social posts. That means seventy people took the time to learn about my employer and decide if they were a technical fit for an open position and a cultural fit with the company. Some of these people I know, some were referred by my contacts, and others discovered the social post on their own through network effects.

In this chapter, my goal is to empower you as an employer to find a university's services as useful as I have. Here are a handful of tips to engage with your university's community:

Put Yourself Out There (Online)

- Post internships and entry-level jobs and host virtual career fairs to students at more than 1,200 universities through Handshake, a job platform targeted to students and young alumni. It is open to any employer and has 550,000 employers, including 100 percent of the Fortune 500, represented on the website.
- Post micro-internships (short-term projects) to students through Parker Dewey, a job platform targeting short-term gigs for students. It is also open to any employer and projects can range from a few hours to several weeks. Parker Dewey differentiates itself by not disclosing the employer to the student until they are matched for a micro-internship.
- Build and maintain a strong digital presence as a company on social media channels, including LinkedIn and Twitter, as this reflects your company's brand. As an employer, you should educate your employees that their social media profiles reflect on the company too.
- Ask the university if they use a hashtag on career posts to add them to your social posts for discoverability. At GW, it was #hiregw.

Link up on LinkedIn

- Start discussions in the LinkedIn group for your university's alumni to discover thought leaders. These LinkedIn groups, if set up right, should include the university's ecosystem of alumni, students, faculty, staff, and parents to maximize participation.
- Grow your professional network by encouraging students to reach out to you with questions about their major, student clubs, or next steps. Sharing your affinities with the students helps them to find commonalities, especially if you choose to leave off information on your college major or class year on your LinkedIn profile.

Put Yourself Out There (Physically)

- Participate in careers fairs held on campus and virtually to bring interest to your company.
- Get involved with the university's employer relations office to speak at an information session or as a panelist at an industry-focused event.

Make the Most of Face Time

- Host one-on-one, employer-in-residence office hours on campus or virtually to find students interested in your employer or your career path.
- Volunteer to mock interview students before a career fair.
- Arrange a site visit at your office for interested students that showcases a few different entry-level roles, other alumni's career paths, and perhaps, a job shadow component.

HIRING LANDSCAPE

To get a sense of today's market, I spoke with Shawn VanDerziel, executive director of the National Association of Colleges and Employers (NACE), a professional membership association made up of 9,300 college and university career services professionals, 3,400 recruiting professionals from multiple sectors, and three hundred business solution providers. After leading a rigorous three-year strategic planning process as a board member, VanDerziel stepped into this NACE leadership role in spring 2020.

We spoke at his one-year mark reflecting on the changes made by the member organizations during the COVID-19 pandemic. VanDerziel sets the scene: "Students and their parents are expecting a higher touch from universities. Most students go to college because there is a promise of a return on your investment, and typically, that return on investment is getting a really good job. What the virtual world produced for us and proved out was that the expectations from students and parents have become even higher. Every university is looking for their differentiator: where are their alumni, how are they measuring career outcomes, and where are their students landing successfully. These questions are going to continue to be asked in a more pressurized way."

On the flip side, US employers faced similar pressures in 2020 not only due to the pandemic, but with the social justice issues that came into the media spotlight. VanDerziel saw the employers' recruiting patterns change as he settled into his new job, explaining, "Previously, employers had a group of target schools, but with the expansion of virtual possibilities across universities and colleges in the US, employers expanded their ability to reach students they were unable to tap into previously, particularly marginalized and under-served students. Also, they are able to communicate and get themselves in front of students in a different way."

"They were able to adapt," VanDerziel said to describe how universities, "for the most part, really continued their career programming just in a virtual method. So, by and large, almost every service that they did in person, they continued in a virtual world, and then some." Some schools were slower to adapt as they put the right technology in place, mainly virtual career platforms, but most could leverage existing tools from within the university, such as video conferencing tools, for their virtual events by fall 2020.

Given dialogue with both universities and employers informed VanDerziel's perspective, he viewed the hybrid approach to career services, including virtual career fairs, virtual information sessions, virtual interviewing, and vir-tual internships, continuing for the next couple of years due to "the reach and the value that's provided in virtual services. It translates into high touch interactions with students and expands the employer-student connection. That is critically important." With the barrier lowered to reach more students through digital means, VanDerziel pointed out, "recruiters can reach that many more students if the university lets them meet virtually with their students. Now, the recruiter gains access to great students that could be employed by their firm. Therefore, the career center needs to provide more opportunity for their students and more exposure to their students." As a result of the shifts made during the 2019–21 academic years, college students may continue to benefit from expanded access to on-campus recruiting for the 2021–23 academic years.

Employers also became savvier in finding employee success stories, tracking their schools and majors, then digging into their alumni networks, especially in the science, technology, engineering, and math (STEM) fields. Then, as the employer targets a particular school, they ask staff, typically school alumni who are outside of the recruiting team, to speak with students as part of on-campus recruitment.

Universities continue to evolve the technology stack to serve students and employers. Students, parents, and employers can expect universities to provide these types of tools, including, but not limited to:

- software to connect students with employers
- mobility tool for students to search visa and employer requirements in other countries
- interview preparation software
- peer to peer reviews of internships or employers
- career search and networking opportunities
- video interviewing software that can be leveraged by small to medium-sized businesses to meet students
- virtual career fair platforms
- resume review software
- mentoring systems to connect with alumni or mentors

Besides the tools and programming, universities are offering for-credit courses on career management techniques. VanDerziel predicts a rise in this offering, commenting, "More and more colleges and universities are offering services both by faculty and the career service departments on those career search processes and integrating successful career navigation techniques within the context of for-credit courses." For example, GW's School of Business offers a one-credit course called "Career Management Strategy," where the instructor, Julianna Hutchins, is a career coach from the Center. Over thirteen weeks, students earn class points by becoming familiar with the career resources offered by the school, compiling a target list of contacts, and presenting their elevator pitch to the class.

Most major colleges and universities have a career center to stay competitive in the market. In NACE's latest benchmark report, they surveyed universities to find that 72 percent of career centers offer alumni outreach. Three out of four universities can help students after they graduate with their job search. That is a powerful statistic. While they may not be able to offer a robust set of tools or a dedicated resource, VanDerziel shared, "There may be some level of connection that they can offer. Or they want to connect with their alumni to understand what they are doing career wise, to help alumni connect back with campus, or make connections between current students and alumni." As far as the 28 percent of career centers without alumni outreach, VanDerziel commented, "Not all colleges and universities are created equal. It's simply resources. Priorities are different, especially with smaller universities and colleges."

DIGITAL TOOLS FOR EMPLOYERS

On the digital side, VanDerziel recognized "social media is important for employers from a branding perspective and to raise awareness—not just from a product and services perspective, but from a prospective employee perspective. Students are busy checking out potential employers on social media." Students place value on being able to find out about an employer and their work environment on the social channels comfortable to them, like Instagram, TikTok, or Twitter. This also means they are more comfortable sharing when they find a job with their social networks. VanDerziel noted, "In this COVID world, the examples of students—really people in general—obtaining jobs through Twitter, LinkedIn, and virtual networking has risen exponentially. A lot more people are posting about the fact they found their jobs in those places than ever before."

In the software that connects students with employers, company representatives can post job or internship openings that may also appear on their own career websites or LinkedIn. The university job portals serve as a warm handshake between the university and employer, then the employer and the student, to which VanDerziel agreed: "Those platforms are fantastic because the employers know they are going to reach the students they want. Employers are able to target students by degree type or academic year. Students can also drill down on these vetted employers."

PARTNERING WITH UNIVERSITIES

GW's Center for Career Services (the Center) award-winning programming completely shaped my view of an employer's engagement with a university and its constituents. This is an account of the numerous ways they are able to bring employers to campus both before and during the pandemic.

The employer services department is run by Managing Director Staci Fowler. She organizes her team of employer development consultants by industry, so that employers have a liaison to understand the array of students they can interact with and perhaps, secure warm referrals for open roles. They complement the Center's industry coaches. Students are not restricted to meet with an industry coach. For example, Fowler recalled, "An American history major wanted to work in media and communications, so they were welcome to schedule a meeting with the media and communications coach." The employer development consultants also work closely with the career coaches that help students to prepare for their career and job search processes. For example, Steve Scordo, the STEM employer development consultant paired up with Sonya Merrill, the STEM career coach. Together, they launched an online job boot camp for smaller groups of ten to twenty students, where Merrill guided the students on their narrative and resume, while Scordo provided the employer landscape. Fowler recognized the importance of community for the students, sharing, "They can't do these things on their own."

Fowler sought unique internship opportunities for the GW students. When a member of the university's strong alumni community approached her office about arranging an exclusive internship program with the Partnership for Public Service, a nonprofit organization oriented around public service careers, the Center was able to set up five paid internships every year reserved for GW students on Handshake. As an employer, you can also carve out internships affiliated with the local college to deepen that relationship between institutions. It creates an ongoing pipeline of talent from the college to your firm.

At the start of the COVID-19 pandemic, Fowler saw formal, on-site internships disappear from Handshake, so her team introduced Parker Dewey's micro-internship platform to the students. She described the need for the switch: "With students virtual, working on Capitol Hill wasn't necessarily an option. So how can students still get skills during the pandemic? Micro-internships existed before the pandemic and we saw an opportunity for them at GW." Over seven hundred students discovered micro-internships to work with large companies on confidential projects or professors seeking help on research initiatives. Given the volume of students able to work virtually on the platform and employers' needs constantly shifting (no project is too small), Fowler advised students to "check the site daily to see what is posted and apply."

The suite of online tools evolved as the pandemic dragged on, enabling Fowler and her team to shift well-orchestrated, in-person events with over a hundred employers to a virtual format. For example, Handshake launched virtual career fairs within their platform. For Fowler's team, they can now see data on how much time a student spends wandering around the employer stands or which virtual booths are popular with students, which is a game changer because "we did not know which student spoke with which employer in a traditional career fair." I echo her point—as an employer, I found it difficult to maintain a sign-in sheet at the company's table because so many would bypass it that I did away with it after my first career fair as an employer. Instead, I asked for a copy of the student or alumnus's resume to keep track of who spoke with me, then I could jot down notes on their resume from our conversation to follow up. I am supportive of a system that tracks these metrics for you.

In the virtual career fair, Handshake tracks the attendees and time spent with each employer for both the university and employer, so they can optimize for future events. Another feature in Handshake's career fair portal is when students opt in to speak with a recruiter, the recruiter sees their profile before they start a conversation, so they can jump past formalities in their short time together. Universities need to prepare students on how to network with employers in a digital space to make the most of the interaction with a positive first impression. Trust me, it is not the same as an in-person event!

Another way employers can engage with a university is by meeting with faculty to inform their curriculum. The idea stemmed from annual meetings held by the employer services team with the deans of the schools within GW. In one of these meetings, the former associate dean of GW's Milken Institute for Public Health asked Fowler's team about employers' thoughts on their curriculum. As a result, they facilitated this type of dialogue with the associate dean, the school's academic units, and a few employers, as well as local alumni from employers. The alumni's firsthand examples of "this class in particular helped me in my job" served as powerful testimonials to the other meeting participants, resulting in changes to the school's resume guide and a public health course's curriculum.

The pandemic has also opened virtual doors to alumni that were previously unable to participate in the university's on-campus programming. For example, Fowler's office used to host a student trek program called "GW Career Quest" to New York City and major US cities for site visits and job shadowing. It required applications, interviews, and a selection process that limited access for a small group of students interested in participating on the trip during summer, fall, or winter break. Now, they offer a virtual careers panel featuring alumni in Atlanta, GA, Los Angeles, CA, San Francisco, CA, and Seattle, WA, throughout the year, attracting sixty students per session. They also bring alumni into programming by inviting them to speak in a class. When one of the employers from the GW Career Quest still wanted to interact with the students, they were invited to speak to a journalism class online.

At the time of our conversation, Fowler arranged a round-table discussion for GW's Center for Professional Studies and three employers with headquarters in the Washington, DC, metro area in spring 2021. According to Fowler, the meeting originated from conversations where the faculty "wanted to hear from employers not only about internship opportunities, but ways to revise their curriculum to ensure they're preparing students for skills in the job market." Her outreach targeted employers who her team is in constant contact with, but also, employers that do not recruit from the university. By providing the opportunity for information sharing, she hoped they would see the university in a different light and choose to recruit students or alumni in the future. She concluded, "With this outreach, we are not saying to these employers to make GW into a target school, but we are saying we want our students to be competitive, so that when they do apply to your company, they have the skill set that you are looking for."

Finally, the pandemic rallied together the universities in the Washington, DC, metro area like never before. Previously, a local employer would have to travel to each university's on-campus career events throughout the academic year, but now, the universities banded together to create a series of virtual events on Handshake for their joint employers, open to students from the consortium of universities, including GW, American University, George Mason University, Georgetown University, Howard University, Johns Hopkins University, and University of Maryland. Fowler sees this collective outlasting the pandemic.

As far as what's next for the progressive Employer Relations office at GW, Fowler foresees "a big push on understanding employer's diversity and inclusion (D&I) programming." According to Monster's *The Future of Work* 2021 survey, "More than one in three global employers don't have a D&I strategy in place. But the good news is nearly half are working on it." She internalized this shift as "not only thinking from the programming perspective, but also thinking about from being more intentional... sort of vetting an employer's understanding about what does D&I mean to them and how that is communicated to students before they apply for the job on Handshake." Monster concluded "45 percent of candidates expect to learn about a company's diversity and inclusion efforts. Employees want: inclusive work environments and workspaces, having people from diverse backgrounds in leadership positions, and encouraging employee resource groups." As they look forward to the 2021–22 academic year, I expect to see this manifest in both how her office communicates with the employers, and in turn, how the students receive communications from these employers.

PARTNERING WITH GRADUATE SCHOOLS

Graduate schools within a university are likely to have their own career center, especially business schools. Students and alumni of these programs should facilitate their relationships with these graduate-school specific career centers before and after graduation. As I shared in Chapter 1, I could not leverage the MIT Sloan Career Development Office (CDO) as a student, but I plugged into their offerings as an alumna and hiring manager since summer 2017. This is how graduate schools bring employers to campus both in person and virtually.

The MIT Sloan CDO is run by Susan Brennan, assistant dean of career development. In her role, she serves on each of the policy committees for each of the degree programs, discussing curriculum, enrollment, and market trends. The CDO supports seven business school degree programs, with different sets of student profiles and target employers. Brennan advised, "When you think of the complexity of this portfolio, how we think of the programming is contextual—there is advising, coaching and instructional design." Their overall framework consists of individual advisors, curriculum, and employer programs. She also recognized, "The journey that we've been on from 2018 has been thinking about how technology could help us to move from transaction to transformation to help us to scale. Of course, we're MIT, so how do we use artificial intelligence to be able to actually do more transformational work?"

The CDO approaches student advising in a multi-layered approach that includes students, alumni, and CDO coaches. First, they selected and trained fifty second-year MBA students to serve as peer coaches, more formally known as MBA Core Fellows, to the first-year students as they arrive on-campus. From the testimonials listed in the CDO's annual magazine, students indicated the value of Core Fellows mentorship in introductions, class selection, and resume reviews. As Brennan described it, "This new initiative stemmed from our students' focus on peer reviews because getting that inside scoop from this network is more trustworthy."

The next level of advising comes from fifty MIT Sloan alumni, who volunteer as industry advisors. Brennan explained, "They provide a next level of expert advice." Employers can seek out these types of advising opportunities for their employees to recommend them. Finally, the CDO has a team of eighteen full-time and part-time career coaches that are assigned to particular degree programs or bring industry expertise to advise students. "We play more of a curator, connector role for the students," said Brennan about the structure, continuing, "Even our online platform is arranged by career communities, so we have a way to easily connect curriculum, student clubs, and other content."

Starting in summer 2018, Brennan and team worked with the faculty to reimagine the career core course taught through a partnership of the CDO and the school's communications faculty to the MBA students starting at their orientation. A new industry-focused series called "Steering Your Career" encouraged first-year students to learn about various career pathways. During the COVID-19 pandemic, she accelerated the work as she described, "We've brought one of our team members into a central role to think about how we can customize the curriculum based upon each program's needs." By fall 2020, her team launched career programming for the mid-career and executive MBA students.

"Fifty percent of the MBA students took jobs with the top twenty companies, but the other half joined first time employers. Are we as innovative as the MIT ecosystem?" questioned Brennan. The recruiting landscape changed and the CDO needed to adjust their strategy. In an effort to keep up with the students' requests, the CDO applied Jeff Bussgang's *Entering StartUpLand* model to their recruiting process, segmenting companies to target into three categories:

- highway = larger companies that hire cohorts of students a year in advance;
- dirt road = 'tween startups in growth stage;
- jungle = early-stage startups, including those being created on campus.

As an alumna, I can vouch for an increasing number of "dirt road" startups appearing on their daily newsletter. The team stays informed on the types of companies to approach by relying on career interest surveys completed by students, examining employment reports from recent alumni, and industry publications listing the best startups.

Mark Newhall is the director of employer relations and recruiting on the CDO team. He stepped into the role right at the start of the pandemic, switching the entire model from in-person to virtual for three hundred employers and more than one thousand students. In spring 2020, the school sent two emails to alumni for virtual summer internships and sourced over two hundred opportunities, including regular and micro-internships.

The MIT Sloan students in the 2020–21 academic year experienced a completely virtual recruiting cycle from their homes around the world. While some students made it to Cambridge, MA, everyone participated in the programming through the Remo virtual event platform or GradLeaders virtual career fairs platform. Newhall reflects on the employers' willingness to adapt: "The feedback has been really positive because from a networking perspective, it's very efficient. They don't need to hop on a plane, book a hotel and conference room. Instead, they can hop on our virtual platforms to meet with students and answer their questions." He also shared that the virtual opportunities attracted employers who previously would not fly in for on-campus recruiting, but now, could participate in virtual sessions.

While all parties are pleased with the school's shift to virtual, Newhall is quick to point out, "I think that it will slightly change in upcoming years. There will be a core set of employers who want to be on campus, likely the more established 'highway companies,' with traditional career paths and hiring cohorts." Based on *The Future of Work* employer survey, Monster indicates retail, leisure/hospitality, real estate, healthcare, manufacturing, and business services may "rely on old-school recruiting."

"We anticipate a large number of companies who will want to continue to present and host coffee chats virtually, but some companies may prefer to host interviews in person. To some extent, the students may drive the in person experience because they miss the in person interaction with the company representatives after the event. In a virtual session, everyone signs off and goes on their way." According to Monster, "While it may offer a safe, and socially distant way of meeting with prospective hires, both employers and candidates (Gen Z in particular) are finding virtual recruiting a challenge for getting a true feel for culture and value alignment, and it's a particular pain point for small and medium-sized businesses."

The CDO team meets monthly with their counterparts at peer schools. Students that cross-register between schools can take advantage of both job boards through reciprocity within the group. Newhall observed, "The pandemic effectively created opportunities to be more collaborative. There was an increase in multi-school events this past year, with a banding together of peer schools for two multi-school career fairs. Each school brought a couple of employers to the event." Recently, the CDO launched an alumni survey to the classes of 2010 and 2015 to better understand the career competencies of these graduates in the workplace and identify the gaps. With that survey data, Brennan hoped "they can feed those powerful insights back to faculty to reverse-engineer the whole process." She also encouraged the peer schools to be more involved in the alumni survey to accumulate better benchmark data. According to Ashley Lautzenheiser of the Forté Foundation, "Employers can look at the school's employment report to see where students may be going instead of your firm."

CONCLUSION

As employers adjust their recruiting strategies as countries emerge from the COVID-19 pandemic, they should definitely leverage universities to augment their talent pipelines. There is an abundance of talent, especially when employers can align their most successful employees' profiles to their previous employers or universities to hire similar profiles, then they can organically find people with transferable skills that are a fit for their organization.

CHAPTER NINETEEN

GUIDE TO YOUR LINKEDIN PROFILE

———

WHEN TO GET STARTED

There are three opportune moments to create a LinkedIn profile:

The minimum age to join LinkedIn is sixteen years old, so high school students can develop their online portfolios in their junior year. This step can help them to organize their online persona before the college admissions process begins, guiding them to craft their narrative for admissions essays. Natasha Singer of *The New York Times* recognized the importance of the LinkedIn profile at this age: "Some high school students are establishing LinkedIn profiles to give the colleges that do look something they would like them to find." Also, it can also enable them to find, connect, and follow-up on informational interviews with alumni for the universities they are interested in.

The next logical time to set up a LinkedIn profile is during a student's first semester of college. University students should professionalize their digital presence as soon as they step foot on campus. LinkedIn allows students to highlight their education and coursework as they search for internships, work-study, or part-time jobs. Singer explained it as "coaching students to build online resumes may increase their sense of agency." Then, as a student secures internships and leadership roles in student organizations, they can add this information to their LinkedIn profile each semester. Finally, by the time they are seeking a full-time job or applying to graduate school, the student's LinkedIn profile serves as their professional calling card to recruiters or admissions representatives.

If you are already in the workforce, you can populate your LinkedIn profile to showcase your professional accomplishments. As you progress in your career, you may find your resume has limited real estate, but no one minds scrolling up and down a LinkedIn profile. This online portfolio can be robust, featuring your experiences and multimedia, including photos, videos and other content, to paint a more complete picture of who you are.

YOUR PROFILE

The most important digital tool to show your transferable skills is your LinkedIn profile. Many folks will find that setting up the sections of a LinkedIn profile to be straightforward, especially since LinkedIn has an "add profile section" wizard that guides you through each section to populate your profile and earn an "All Star" badge. The top five sections to complete are Intro, About, Experience, Education, and Volunteer experience.

The About section on a LinkedIn profile shows the candidate's interests, passions, and achievements in their own words. It can also connect the dots between nonlinear experiences, highlight the skills that the candidate is proud of, and show off their personality, like Simone Williams accomplished in her narrative.

PROFILE SECTIONS

You can find many resources about completing your LinkedIn profile, including checklists from LinkedIn circulating on the Internet. For example, they distinguish how high school or college students should populate their profile, with more robust detail required from the college student's profile:

LinkedIn Profile Checklists for Students

LinkedIn Section	High School Student	College Student
EDUCATION	Starting with high school, list all the educational experiences you've had, including summer programs.	Starting with college, list all the educational experiences you've had, including summer programs; can include GPA, awards and honors if recent and/or relevant.
VOLUNTEER EXPERIENCES	Even if you weren't paid for a job, be sure to list it. Admissions officers and employers often see volunteer experience as valuable as paid work.	Even if you weren't paid for a job, be sure to list it. Admissions officers and employers often see volunteer experience as valuable as paid work; add personality and passion to your profile, show involvement.
PROJECTS	Whether you led a team assignment in school or built an app on your own, talk about what you did and how you did it.	Whether you led a team assignment in school or built an app on your own, talk about what you did and how you did it; great area to include other relevant professional or academic experiences; tag teammates.
ORGANIZATIONS	Have you joined any clubs at school or outside? Be sure to describe what you did with each organization.	Have you joined any clubs at school or outside? Be sure to describe what you did with each organization; campus/external involvement showcases additional skills and interests.

Source: LinkedIn Profile Checklists for University and High School

PHOTOS

You can make a good first impression of your LinkedIn profile with your headshot photo and background photo. Many articles recommend using color images for both photos, with LinkedIn's own data highlighting that a profile with a headshot receives twenty-one times more clicks in LinkedIn search results and nine times more connection requests, so it is a good way to distinguish yourself from others.

Make sure your headshot photo is current—one to three years old maximum. If you do not have a photo and need one, ask a friend or family member to take one from the shoulders up in front of a plain wall or outdoors in natural light. Also, if you are affiliated with your alma mater, they may offer photo booths with free headshots at university events including career fairs, class reunions, or larger gatherings such as conferences. For the past eight years, I have taken advantage of the university option to refresh my headshot every few years. A high-quality local photographer takes eight to ten photos of you and sends both the color and black and white versions within a week of the event. Another place that may offer free headshots is your employer. With the last two options, if you have not seen it happen yet, then you can ask. I also update my headshot on all my social channels at the same time, so it makes it easier for someone to find me. It allows someone to recognize you across platforms and becomes more important if you have a common name.

HEADLINE

By default, LinkedIn lists your current role at your current company in this field, which already appears in the

Experience section of your profile. So, you should customize the headline to reflect a mini-elevator pitch to demonstrate your personality. Take advantage of the space (220 characters) to use keywords or short phrases, separated by vertical bars (|), that describe you and your skills.

When someone is actively looking for a job, I recommend that they write "Actively Seeking..." in the headline to make their intentions clear to others. If you are unsure of what to write, type some keywords that interest you into the LinkedIn search bar to see how many other people use the same terms or phrases in their headline.

In my headline, I added my social media handle (it is the same across Twitter and Instagram) for three reasons:

1. It makes it easier to find me on those social media channels.
2. Sometimes the LinkedIn search results truncate your name to show only the first name and last initial, but they always show the full headline. With my social media handle listed, someone can find my full name and reach out to me on either platform.
3. I post more frequently on Twitter, so someone can get a better sense of me on that platform.

LOCATION
LinkedIn did a refresh of its locations in 2020 and continues to add cities to the list, so check yours periodically to make sure it is current. For example, New York City used to appear as Greater New York City Area, then changed to New York City Metropolitan Area. You want to make sure you keep it

current with LinkedIn's latest selections to show up in search results properly.

If you are relocating to a new geographic area, you should update the LinkedIn profile location to reflect the location where you are going to live. This way, you will show up in search results of recruiter's looking for candidates in that geographic area. Furthermore, you can explain in both your LinkedIn profile's About section and in interviews that you are relocating, then see if the employer can include relocation benefits to your compensation package.

PROFILE URL

At the top right of the LinkedIn profile page, there is an extremely important edit button: "Edit public profile & URL." It lets you edit your custom website link from a string of letters and numbers automatically generated by LinkedIn to a more personalized link produced by you. Some unique options are:

- your full name;
- your company name (if you own the company);
- a truncated version of your name and/or company;
- your social media handles.

Then, you can use this customized link on your personal business card, email signature, and resume header. It makes it easier for your profile to be discovered and contributes to your personal brand.

This same "Edit public profile & URL" page also allows you to adjust your public profile settings by the profile section, visibility in and out of LinkedIn, and the ability to generate a badge to add your LinkedIn profile to another website.

All of these changes to your profile help increase your profile strength on LinkedIn, which is visible to you on "Your Dashboard" above "Activity". As you complete each section and add media, your profile strength will increase to All-Star. At one point, LinkedIn notified me my profile ranked in the top 4 percent for profile views among my connections, which also feeds into their algorithm and can push you to the top of other's search results.

Now, I'll delve into the key sections of the LinkedIn profile, so that you join me at All-Star status by the end of this chapter.

ABOUT

You can use the About section to craft a narrative to explain your professional and personal journeys beyond the resume bullets. Many of us have non-traditional career paths, which may look confusing both on LinkedIn's Experience section and our resume to others. However, the About section allows you to explain your pivots, connect the dots the reader may not see, and most importantly, explain where you want to go.

In 2013, I watched a four-minute clip about Daniel H. Pink's book entitled *Always Be Selling* that stuck with me. He highlights six different pitch types to help you to get organized, especially since not everything works for everyone in the same way. My favorite to help write the About section is the

Pixar Pitch because it helps you to craft your narrative and build your story. It organizes your story chronologically, with how you went from point A to point B to point Z, explaining the pivots and what you learned. People can read it to get a better sense of who you are in a storytelling format.

Once upon a time _____. Every day _____.
One day _____. Because of that, _____.
Because of that, _____. Until finally, _____.

In my example below, I wrote about my first two major work experiences in the Pixar Pitch format in spring 2013, then stylized it for the LinkedIn About section. I chose not to highlight two minor work experiences because they did not add value to the story.

Once upon a time *at CEB, I guided senior corporate executives in making the best use of our products and services to improve their organizations.*

Every day *I found new and better ways to share client updates and helped my colleagues strengthen their sales conversations. I developed dashboards and templates that could be easily populated with consolidated product information; these became standard CEB offerings.*

One day *I had the opportunity of a lifetime to serve my local government. I contributed to the intersection of government, politics, and technology in enhancing the lives of Washington, DC, residents. I streamlined intra-agency and inter-agency processes to improve service delivery, reallocated resources to ensure program outcomes were delivered*

on time, and encouraged colleagues to productize their
services during tough budget times.

Because of that, *I'm poised to lead the operations of a*
growing start-up or small business. I want to leverage
my expertise to lead the right organization to recruit and
retain the best talent, bridge the sales and technical teams
to make better products, and maintain high levels of cus-
tomer service across the board.

Because of that, *I thrive in entrepreneurial environments*
that welcome operational change, foster meritocracy, and
inspire self-starters to jump out of their lanes.

Until finally, *I am looking for a new role that will leverage*
what I have learned.

With some wordsmithing, I structured the Pixar Pitch for my
career journey into a catchy About section on my LinkedIn
profile.

I thrive in entrepreneurial environments that welcome
operational change, foster meritocracy, and inspire
self-starters to jump out of their lanes.

At CEB, I guided senior corporate executives in making the best use of our products and services to improve
their organizations. Every day, I found new and better
ways to share client updates and helped my colleagues
strengthen their sales conversations. I developed dashboards and templates that could be easily populated with

consolidated product information; these became standard CEB offerings.

I had the opportunity of a lifetime to serve my local government. I contributed to the intersection of government, politics, and technology in enhancing the lives of Washington, DC, residents. I streamlined intra-agency and inter-agency processes to improve service delivery, reallocated resources to ensure program outcomes were delivered on time, and encouraged colleagues to productize their services during tough budget times.

Now, I'm poised to lead the operations of a growing start-up or small business. I want to leverage my expertise to lead the right organization to recruit and retain the best talent, bridge the sales and technical teams to make better products, and maintain high levels of customer service across the board.

You need me on your team. Let's connect.

FEATURED

LinkedIn spotlighted media as part of the Summary section, then pulled it into its own section. I prefer this look because previously, the media was not visible to viewers of your profile. You can add videos, articles, and static documents that are uploaded onto LinkedIn.

This is prime real estate on your LinkedIn profile, so you want it to look good. Please make sure a thumbnail appears for each media content. If one does not appear, you can upload an image to appear in its place. This thumbnail will catch a profile reader's attention to help them to learn more about you.

EXPERIENCE

Following the first section with your name, photo, and headline, Experience is the most important section on LinkedIn. Similar to your resume, it highlights your professional experience in a standardized format that is searchable within the LinkedIn platform. For that reason, it is key to use common terms in each of the fields in this Experience section, so that recruiters and others can find you. You want to fill in every single field available to you, including:

- Company name;
- Your title (or if you had multiple titles in an organization, the most recent);
- Years that you worked at this company;
- Location;
- Description;
- Media and awards.

As I shared earlier in this chapter, when I receive a resume as a hiring manager, the first thing I do is go to LinkedIn to verify the candidate's information. I check that the dates and descriptions match up to validate that a candidate did what they said they did. After all, LinkedIn is a public place where your colleagues can see your profile, so you are less likely to inflate your role and accomplishments in this digital square. That said, please make sure the details from your resume align with your LinkedIn profile.

As you enter the data in the Company name field, LinkedIn will try to match it to a Company in their database. This is what you want to see (with the company icon showing up in your profile), so your profile is connected to the company's page. In the future, if the company gets acquired or changes its name, LinkedIn will keep it up to date on your profile. For example, if you work in an industry with frequent mergers and acquisition (M&A) activity like legal, where you see law firms merging and changing names frequently, then your profile presents the latest information. Also, if someone is searching for a certain type of profile for a hire, you will show up in the search results of past employees for that company and look more favorable to the recruiter.

If you have multiple current professional experiences listed in the Experience section, for example, some people choose to list every experience for work, volunteer activities, and school in this section (versus their own sections), then choose to reorder the experiences in the order that you prefer. You want to make sure the dates go in an order that makes sense chronologically or prioritize your full-time employment over others. Also, there are search-related benefits to listing the school in the Education section, versus the Experience section, that you will read about in the Education & School pages section.

My advice with the LinkedIn profile's Experience section is to not restrict yourself with the content. With a resume, you are limited to one page for every five years of experience and in some cases, such as graduate school applications, you should have one page for up to ten years of experience. With the LinkedIn profile, you can be more verbose in the description and add media and awards to show the depth and breadth of your accomplishments. Viewers of your profile will not mind scrolling up and down your profile whereas they mind seeing a resume longer than the guidelines recommend. Also, the more content may also mean the higher likelihood your profile contains a keyword someone is searching for on the site.

CONNECTIONS

When you are growing your network and asking to connect with someone on LinkedIn, you are asking them to be part of your network (and you theirs). I encourage you to use the "Connect" button on the desktop version of LinkedIn, versus the mobile app. When you click "Connect" on the mobile version, it sends a generic, automated request to the person. If you take an extra step to click on the three-dot menu on a person's profile, then the mini-menu shows an option to "Personalize invite," where you can write a note.

On the desktop version of LinkedIn, you can customize the request to each person, using this opportunity to remind the person of where or how you met, a commonality, or what you are going to do moving forward. You do not want someone to dismiss your request as a spam outreach or because they did not remember you.

Michael Steelman, director of alumni career management and professional networks at William & Mary, reinforced the personalization of LinkedIn connection requests. He shares, "The key thing is, even if it's someone that you know very well, it's always nice to say hello in a more personalized way.

Stand out by including a note with your connection request and it will also help you to keep track of your connections."

He goes so far as to not accepting connection requests without a personalized message right away. Instead, he responds to the connection request by stating, "Thanks for the connection request. Let's find a time to chat and see where we can help one another." Those that take him up on the offer also stand out in their networking abilities.

My recommendation is to send a connection request within twenty-four hours of meeting, so that both you and your interaction are still top of mind for the other person. Steelman suggests a personal note like, "Hi [First Name], it's great to see you're on here. I look forward to connecting and bringing our networks together."

This is a great time to review the pile of business cards sitting on your desk and to add those contacts into LinkedIn, so you can find them more easily. If someone lists their mobile on the business cards, you may want to enter the phone number into your phone's address book before you throw away the card.

I did this exercise myself in spring 2013, where I reviewed eighty-nine business card contacts to add them to LinkedIn. I found 78 percent of those contacts on LinkedIn and the other 18 percent did not have a LinkedIn profile. Since then, I aim to add contacts on LinkedIn within twenty-four hours, so I do not maintain a business card pile.

LINKEDIN GROUPS

Another neat feature is LinkedIn groups, which are created by members for members. They are self-organized, with some groups open to anyone that joins and others restricting membership due to affiliation. When someone chooses to join a LinkedIn group, they are likely active on LinkedIn; they want to be part of a virtual community and connect with others in that community.

Some groups you can join are interest groups, your university's group for students and alumni, and your current or past employer's alumni groups. You can join up to one hundred groups. By posting or commenting in these LinkedIn groups, you build credibility towards your personal brand. You can post articles, job postings, events, and thought-provoking prompts, so other group members will remember you as a thought leader.

During the COVID-19 pandemic in fall 2020, Sarah Harel transitioned from a consultant to a new full-time chief of staff role at the International Centre for Missing and Exploited Children, a nonprofit with a mission to protect children. She worked closely with the CEO and leadership team, but no other person in the firm had a similar role. She shares, "I joined different LinkedIn groups of chiefs of staff to be part of a like-minded community," and gained exposure to people in similar roles at much larger Fortune 500 companies. On the message boards, she posted questions related to her day-to-day work and received "big company answers informed by external market research," which provided a different level of perspective than what she could access. One of her group posts even resulted in an outreach from a distant relative in a similar role at a startup, who recognized Harel's name and offered to help with her question. Harel also found it helpful to attend targeted webinars "that are very specific to what I do," which she learned about from the LinkedIn groups.

Within the group, you can message other group members you are not connected to directly. This is a huge benefit and privilege of participating in the LinkedIn group. This is powerful in connecting with others that share a commonality. You can message them sharing that you are both part of the same LinkedIn group. Otherwise, you would have to send a blind connection request that may not be accepted by the other person or purchase premium features to send an InMail, which is a messaging feature for those who are not connected with each other. Remember that group messaging is a free feature offered by LinkedIn, which they are constantly tweaking. Before LinkedIn provided unlimited messages in this setting for you to take advantage of, now, you can only send fifteen messages per month within a group. So, if you are trying to grow your network, you are relocating or planning to, or you are looking for business development opportunities, then plan how to use your allotted messages each month wisely.

EDUCATION & SCHOOL PAGES

Based on the Education section in our profiles, LinkedIn generated the alumni section of the School pages to bring together those alumni in a searchable format within the platform. Similar to how you want to make sure that the Company page aligns to your employer's name in the Experience section, you want the School Page to align to your educational institution's name in your Education section of your LinkedIn profile. Then, your profile becomes searchable as part of the alumni on a School Page. If you list more than three schools in your Education section, you appear on the School Page as an alumnus for the first three schools listed.

This is a more robust listing of school alumni than the LinkedIn group because it is based on who entered the school's name in the Education section. In a LinkedIn group, LinkedIn users opt to join the group, so it is a subset of the total population that could be in that group.

	LinkedIn group page	School page
MIT Sloan School of Management Alumni	9,664	40,523
The George Washington University Alumni	36,516	167,339

As you can see in the table above, both the MIT Sloan business school alumni and George Washington University alumni LinkedIn groups represent 20 percent of the total alumni present on LinkedIn (as evidenced by the School page counts). That means one in five alumni of these universities that use LinkedIn chose to participate in the active community of the LinkedIn group.

On the School page, where it has its own navigation menu under the school's name, you can see the alumni associated with this institution. Based on their LinkedIn profiles, you can search for them by years of attendance, location, current employer, skills, and degrees of connection. This is a helpful way to search, especially if you are seeking an informational interview about the school before you apply, researching a particular company for a role or business development opportunity, or relocating and want to meet people in your destination city. You can click on the searchable attributes to filter down the list of alumni that appear in the results. Then, you can send a connection request or find them in the LinkedIn group for school alumni to send a message with a customized note referencing you are both alumni of the same school. The shared experience of attending the same school is a powerful commonality, no matter when you graduated, and you are more likely to receive a response compared to a blind outreach.

SOCIAL ENGAGEMENT

Once you build a strong profile and community on LinkedIn, you have to dip your toes into social engagement with other LinkedIn members. This engagement feeds into LinkedIn's algorithm, which I hinted at earlier. Like other social channels, LinkedIn watches your activity, including updates to your profile, self-created posts, and your engagement with others' posts.

You can see how LinkedIn measures your activity on the site, by looking up your Social Selling Index (SSI). Originally created as a business tool, it is available to all LinkedIn users. The four factors of the SSI score are: establish your professional brand, find the right people, engage with insights, and build insights. As you create a network of the "right people," I recommend you accept one LinkedIn connection request per day. That way, you grow your network in a steady pace and demonstrate daily activity. The score is refreshed daily, so you should see the effects of your profile changes within a week.

In her TedXFergusonLibrary Talk, Sandra Long encouraged, "Be the best friend you can be. Do it first and pay it forward... congratulate people, comment on their posts, introduce someone, and show gratitude. All of those things you can do very easily on LinkedIn."

Harel noticed how I use LinkedIn to tag job searchers in job-related posts from others in my network. This is an easy way to help others searching for new jobs find opportunities they may not be aware of. It also serves as a warm referral between myself, the job candidate, and the job poster, so they learn of each other and can continue the conversation offline.

As you can see, LinkedIn is a powerful tool for your digital presence. It can help you reinforce the personal brand you want to establish (or re-establish) and get you in front of recruiters searching the platform. Finally, it can set you up for success with the one-step "easy apply" button on the job postings available on its job board.

CONCLUSION

___

"All I'm saying is simply this: that all mankind is tied together; all life is interrelated, and we are all caught in an inescapable network of mutuality, tied in a single garment of identity. Whatever affects one directly, affects all indirectly. For some strange reason I can never be what I ought to be until you are what you ought to be. And you can never be what I ought to be until I am what I ought to be—this is the interrelated structure of reality."

—MARTIN LUTHER KING, JR.,
OBERLIN COLLEGE 1965 COMMENCEMENT ADDRESS.

The twenty-five real-life stories of career pivoters documented in this book are representative of hundreds of conversations I held across the past twenty years, stemming from my own curiosity to understand how a person moves from one job to the next. With every conversation, and of course, my own career pivots, the combination of transferable skills and connections propelling them into successful careers was evident. Now, you have salient examples to identify your own transferable skills, potential career paths, and similar people in your networks to help make your move.

FIND YOUR COMMON DENOMINATOR OF TRANSFERABLE SKILLS

The forty-two transferable skills highlighted in the book are symbolic of dozens of skills needed in today's job market. They are part of your common denominator of skills. Each person has their own unique set of skills derived from this list.

Active Listening
Adapting to Change
Business Analysis
Coaching
Collaboration
Communicating to Executives
Compassion
Complex Problem Solving
Consensus-Based Decision-Making
Continuous Improvement
Continuous Learning
Creativity
Critical Thinking
Curiosity
Customer First
Dependability
Determined
Diligence
Discipline
Empathy
Endurance
Facilitation
Fearless Networking
Fellowship
Focus

Influence without Authority
Mentorship
Open-Mindedness
People Management
Proactiveness
Project Management
Performing
Self-Awareness
Self-Care
Sociable
Speaking Up
Storytelling
Team Building
Understanding of Social Media
User Research
Vulnerability
Writing

I provided a wide range to stir your thoughts to surface more transferable skills. You can use the template at the end of this chapter to chart your course and highlight your skills at each pivot. If you need help dissecting your story, I recommend the questions posed by either The Dark Horse Project, Pixar Pitch, or Career Anchors framework. The Career Anchors framework* asks:

- What did you do?
- Why did you do that?
- How did it work out (positive and negative elements)?
- What were your plans and ambitions for the future, at that point?
- What are your career goals now?

These questions were listed with permission of the author and the publisher.

Alternately, you may ask others "What do I do well?" so hearing your strengths in their simpler terms can assist you to describe your characteristics in a common way. While the capabilities we bring to the table are obvious to us, they are not always to others.

Once you clarify your goals and identify your skills, read your resume, LinkedIn profile, and social media profiles to see if they illustrate these transferable skills. If they are not consistent, use this book's examples to govern your updates.

If you want to learn these skills (also known as upskilling), you can use digital technologies. According to the World Economic Forum *Future of Jobs Report*, "Skills around people and culture, content writing, and sales and marketing take only a month or two to learn."

SET AN INTENTION

To get started, this idea of setting an intention or plotting a new career can inspire you from stories like Godbout's, where he planned for years on switching from management consulting to a social impact venture, or Udezue's, where she kept her passion in marketing alive despite working outside of the field for years. The ability to keep an open mind for opportunities, like Farrell, Lynes, or Naik, ensured their plates were always full. While curiosity motivated Matar to dive headfirst into venture capital and Cohen into job training, it helped Eromosele to envision a career path that was unknown to her.

In the workforce, you will find different ways to make a major career pivot, including opportunities within your same company, through a professional contact with another organization or by seeking higher education.

I recommend adopting my "IRON" framework to help you to find clarity in this new path. As the level of difficulty increases in your desired career change, you can lean on your transferable skills to demonstrate your capabilities. You should identify your targets to determine:

Skills: The Common Denominator
IRON Framework

	Level of Difficulty		
	Easy	Intermediate	Difficult
INDUSTRY	stay in your current industry	join an adjacent industry	completely switch industries
ROLE	stay in your current role	increase your responsibility	completely switch roles
ORGANIZATION	stay in your current organization	join an organization in adjacent industry	completely switch industries
NETWORK	existing network can facilitate your switch	secondary connections can help	build a whole new network

Once you compile your goals around the next job, then you must coordinate your outreach into your network. You may decide to leverage techniques like Leighton-Guzman, who vocalized her interest in an adjacent organization, or Holland, who talked about his passions in a way that helped second-degree connections open the door for him. When you find the switch to be more difficult, be encouraged by stories like Gomez Lopez, Nassiri, or Plaster, where graduate school played a key role in their abilities to become more confident leaders. As Winston Churchill said, "Fear is a reaction. Courage is a decision."

RINSE AND REPEAT

"Most will change jobs every two years," Penelope Trunk shared with her blog readers in February 2007. I shared how I updated my resume each semester in college. I recommend reviewing your resume and LinkedIn profile Experience section every six to twelve months to make sure you capture the essence of your work while it is fresh. You can use this time to revisit your transferable skills to see if you strengthened existing ones or if you formed new skills. Then, you can adjust your elevator pitch, so you are always ready to talk about your professional goals and the help you need to reach them.

King's quote made it clear—our actions impact others, as do theirs on us. The formula to career success is what you know *and* who you know. You cannot attempt to make these changes on your own and nor should you. I am here for you, your network is here for you, and connections you have not met yet are waiting to hear from you.

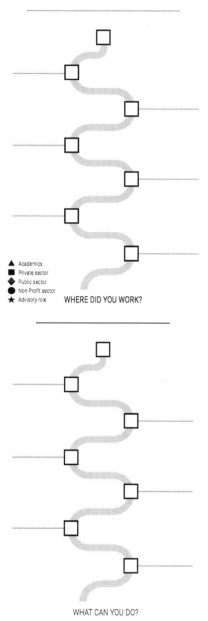

▲ Academics
■ Private sector
◆ Public sector
● Non-Profit sector
★ Advisory role

WHERE DID YOU WORK?

WHAT CAN YOU DO?

GRATITUDE

——

To all those who shared your career stories with me over the years, you left a marked impression on me.

In September 2020, I decided to write this book, which was a surreal process during a once-in-a-lifetime pandemic. Thanks to the Creator Institute and New Degree Press teams for the tested frameworks, constant guidance, and helping hand to structure, write, and publish my first book. Words cannot express my gratitude to my editors, Ashley Alvarez, Christy Mossburg, Emeline Ahn, and Eldar Huseynov, for their professional advice and assistance in polishing this manuscript. Many thanks to Gjorgji Pejkovski, Nikola Tikoski, Liana Morsecu, and the talented art team for perfecting the cover design, infographics, and charts.

Without the experiences and support of my friends and colleagues—old and new—this book would not exist. Thank you to all my interviewees. Thank you for taking time out of your busy schedules to talk to me about your work, the ups and the downs, and most importantly, how you made your career pivots. My goal was to feature real-life stories; this book did not get to where it is without your experiences.

Ana Maria Gomez Lopez
Anjali Naik
Carter Holland
Ejieme Eromosele
Elizabeth Villa
Emily Bosland
Graham Plaster
Jennifer Leighton-Guzman
Jonathan Godbout
Jose Siade
Justin Nassiri
Lindsey Lynes
Loren Cohen
Lynsey Farrell
Mark Newhall

Max Fira*
Michael Steelman
Michelle Udezue
Patrick O'Brien
Pedro Podesta
Sarah Harel
Sasi Yajamanyam
Shawn VanDerziel
Simone Williams
Sonali Batish
Staci Fowler
Susan Brennan
Vijay Swamy
Wassim Matar

I would also like to gratefully acknowledge:

Aditya & Medy Bhat
Ajay & Sonali Batish
Alan & Kim Hanley
Alejandra Gomez Lopez
Alia Abbas
Amit & Nidhi Mahendru
Ana Carolina Freire Gentil
Andrew Bell
Andrew Nebus
Andrew Rhodes
Aneri Shah
Angel Kidka
Annie Wang
Antonio Pepe

Antonio Vargas
Art & Olga Ghazaryan
Ashley Lautzenheiser
Ashna Patel
Auditi Chakravarty
B. & R.P. Aravindakshan
Ben Trajtenberg
Beverly Daly
Bill LePage
Bill Whitson
Bruno & Laila Nogueira
Bryan & Stacey Sivak
Carl Dahlberg
Carlo Mahfouz

Carlo & Novella Perini
Carlos & Celia Carneiro
Carly Rogers
Carolina Cinalli
Carter Holland
Cem & Nippa Esendal
Chris & Nassim Mehrabi
Chris & Kim Willey
Christine Cannon
Dan Haley
Daniel Stern
Dasle Kim
David Gragan
David & Priya Menachery
David Mihalchik
David & Matt Nurnberg
David Smith
Davin Galbraith
Dawinder Sidhu
Deb Welke
Dev Kataria
Diana Godoy
Diane Adams
Dipali Chakravarti
Douglas Hwang
Drew Smith
Ejieme Eromosele
Ekata Doshi
Elli Orth
E. & Sofia Theodoridou
Emily Bosland
Eric Koester

Fardin & Sara Farooq
Fifile Nguyen
Gabriela Millan
Gabrielle Haddad
Gaurav & Anjana Jindal
Gautam Advani
Geo George
Hadrian Sousa
Hema Aravindakshan
Hippolyte Petit
Jamal Mazhar
James Walker
Jamie Bosse
Jason Ireland
Javier & Enisa Canon
Jay & Sejal Patel
Jay Vigeland
Jennifer Leighton-Guzman
Jeremy Gosbee
Jessica Han
Jessica Tunon
Joe Walsh
John Falcicchio
John & Diem Law
Jonathan Godbout
Jose Siade
Joey & Sunitha Mathews
Joseph & Risha George
Joshua & Shejal Carpenter
Juhu Thukral
Julieta Schuster
Julio Ramirez

Jyoti Singhvi

Kalliope Kokolis

Karen Rosner

Karina Mc Entee

Kathy Kim-Juhn

Kathy Lui

Kei & Tomoko Yamashita

Kelly Chen

Kelly Courtney

Krishna Murthy

Krishna Vallabhaneni

KK & Ramya Kodukula

Lara Kataria

Laura Castillo

Laura Tovar & G.Araujo

Laveen Venugopalan

Lawrence Poster

LeRoy Pingho

Leslie & Beena Mathew

Lincy Philip

Lindsey Lynes

Lindsey Vivenzio

Liz Longenecker

Liza Bulos

Lucia Hwang

Luis & Daniella Schio, Jr.

Lynsey Farrell

Manoj Nair

Marcia Call

Maria Botchkova

Mark Tefakis

Marshall Kirkpatrick

Martin Baum

Maruf & Suraiya Haider

Marva Gumbs Jennings

Matt Tedder

Maya Sunil

Melkizedeck Okudo

Micah Beckman

Micha Cooper-Edwards

Michael Steelman

Mital & Shuchi Desai

Mitch Ebin

Monideep & Madhu Nag

Mosum Parikh

Mubuso Zamchiya

Murali Swaminathan

Nancy Novak

Natalia Palmer

Natalie Gil & Silvana Lopez

Naveen Rajdev

Neil & Lynn Kataria

Nicholas Hill

Nikki Harrell

Nobel & Betty Philip

Oshiya Savur

Padma Vanka

Pandwe Gibson

Paru Radia

Patrick O'Brien

Pavan & Mica Thimmaiah

Pedro & Angie Podesta

Pete Francis

Philip Komarny

Pradeep Suthram
Praful & Shreem Ramineni
Raabia Budhwani
Rachel Alvarez
Raj & Morgan Naik
Ravi Subrahmanyan
Rebecca Klemm
Riyadh & Merfat Alomair
Robert Snyder
Rodrigo & Carola Bloomfield
Rosemary Maloney
Roshan & Vipra Polepalli
Roulla Nau
Rudy Seber
Rukshana Karunaratne
Ruth Sommers
Ryan Mathew
Sacha Ghebali
Sameer Acharya
Samir & Anjali Naik
Sarah Harel
Sarah Song
Sarah Sukumaran
Sasi Yajamanyam
Scott Earl
Shaan Kataria
Shanti Aranha
Shaji Joseph
Shaun Bertram
Sheela Sreekumar
Sheinal & Jackie Bhuralal
Sheryl Freeman

Shirley Kwan-Hui
Shyam Chidamber
Sierra Davidson
Sikaar Keita
Simone Williams
Sonika Patel
Srikanth Subramanian
Staci Fowler
Stacy Taylor
Stephanie Chin
Stephanie Whitacre
Steven Frenkil
Sudhakar Ramasamy
Sun Gyu & Hye Young Han
Tafadzwa & Emilia Magaya
Tenzin Youdon
Terry Thomas
Tom Packman
Toufic & Aceil Hirbli
Travis Rapp
Trish Cotter
Victor & Bukky Oisaghie
Vinay & Anjali Bhargava
Vijay & Anitha Balkissoon
Vijay Swamy
Vineet & Meha Narula
Vivek & Sapna Kundra
Wassim & Soraya Matar
Will Reagan
Ximena Hartsock
Zach Boisi
Zoya Haider

Name changed upon request

If you enjoyed reading this book, it would mean the world to me if you wrote a review on Amazon or Goodreads to let me know your thoughts: *https://bit.ly/skillsbookreview.*

APPENDIX

———

INTRODUCTION

Connley, Courtney. "3 signs you're stuck in the wrong career." *Make It* (blog). *CNBC.com*, April 11, 2018. *https://www.cnbc.com/2018/04/11/3-signs-youre-stuck-in-the-wrong-career.html*.

Hoffman, Reid and Ben Casnocha. *The Start-up of You: Adapt to the Future, Invest in Yourself, and Transform Your Career*. New York: Random House, Inc., 2012.

Indeed. "Career Change Report: An Inside Look at Why Workers Shift Gears." October 30, 2019. *https://www.indeed.com/lead/career-change*.

Pink, Daniel H. *Drive: The Surprising Truth About What Motivates Us*. New York: Riverhead Books, 2009.

Productivity Game. "DRIVE by Daniel Pink | Animated Core Message." October 25, 2017. Video, 8:28. *https://youtu.be/_BmH-dTC36N4*.

Stanford News. "'You've got to find what you love,' Jobs says." June 14, 2005. *https://news.stanford.edu/2005/06/14/jobs-061505/*.

SXSW. "The Start-Up of YOU: 21st Century Career Strategy | Interactive 2012 | SXSW." July 26, 2012. Video, 7:29. *https://youtu. be/MX5OZhCtovI.*

CHAPTER ONE—ASHA ARAVINDAKSHAN: MY STORY

"2022 Best Business Schools." *U.S. News & World Report.* February 4, 2021. *https://www.usnews.com/best-graduate-schools/ top-business-schools/mba-rankings.*

Bosland, Emily. "How to Change the World and Still Pay Your Bills." *Ashoka* (blog). *Forbes.* January 22, 2013. *https://www. forbes.com/sites/ashoka/2013/01/22/how-to-change-the-world- and-still-pay-your-bills/.*

Epstein, David. *Range.* New York: Riverhead Books, 2019.

Harvard Graduate School of Education. "The Dark Horse Project." Accessed May 24, 2021. *https://lsi.gse.harvard.edu/dark-horse.*

Phan, Anna. "A Study of the Challenges of Nonlinear Career Changers and a New Services to Ease the Transition." (master's thesis, MIT, 2018) *http://hdl.handle.net/1721.1/118529.*

Productivity Game. "RANGE by David Epstein | Core Message." November 3, 2019. Video, 9:07. *https://youtu.be/p4rP8CGaVDY.*

STORIES OF CAREER REINVENTION

Gilbert, Elizabeth. "Success, failure and the drive to keep creating." Filmed March 2014 at TED, Vancouver, BC. Video, 7:05. *https:// www.ted.com/talks/elizabeth_gilbert_success_failure_and_the_ drive_to_keep_creating#t-417276.*

Heffernan, Margaret. "The human skills we need in an unpredictable world." Filmed July 2019 at TEDSummit, Edinburgh,

Scotland. Video, 15:44. *https://www.ted.com/talks/margaret_heffernan_the_human_skills_we_need_in_an_unpredictable_world.*

Hughes, Neil C. Great TED Talks—Innovation. California: Portable Press, 2020.

CHAPTER TWO—LYNSEY FARRELL: FROM YOUTH ADVOCATE TO ANTHROPOLOGY PROFESSOR

Vioreanu, Dana. "How to Successfully Combine Work with a PhD?" January 6, 2021. *https://www.phdportal.com/articles/1942/how-to-successfully-combine-work-with-a-phd.html.*

CHAPTER THREE—GRAHAM PLASTER: FROM MILITARY DIPLOMAT TO COMMUNITY MANAGER

Keller, Jared. "Evaluating Iran's Twitter Revolution." *The Atlantic.* June 18, 2010. *https://www.theatlantic.com/technology/archive/2010/06/evaluating-irans-twitter-revolution/58337/.*

TEDx Talks. "Creating a culture of collaborative innovation | Claire Madden | TEDxQUT." October 16, 2015. Video, 13:32. *https://youtu.be/vaN6FtJ8inA.*

CHAPTER FOUR—JENNIFER LEIGHTON-GUZMAN: FROM FUNDRAISER TO CHECK WRITER

National Association for College Admission Counseling. "Transfer Students: Recruitment and Admission at Four-Year Colleges." Accessed July 26, 2021. *https://www.nacacnet.org/globalassets/documents/publications/research/socatransfer.pdf.*

CHAPTER FIVE—ANJALI NAIK: FROM MUSIC ENTREPRENEUR TO ROBOTICS ENTREPRENEUR

Forrester. "Playbooks." Accessed July 26, 2021. *https://www.for-rester.com/playbooks#.*

CHAPTER SIX—JUSTIN NASSIRI: FROM NAVAL OFFICER TO CONTENT STRATEGIST

TEDx Talks. "Where are your blindspots? | Noemie Delfassy | TEDxLSE." April 15, 2016. Video, 9:31. *https://youtu.be/JnZmE-HyYojo.*

CHAPTER SEVEN—LOREN COHEN: FROM LAWYER TO JOB TRAINING ENTREPRENEUR

Dugan, Regina. "From Mach-20 Glider to Hummingboard Drone." Filmed February 28, 2012 at TED, Long Beach, CA. Video, 24:43. *https://www.ted.com/talks/regina_dugan_from_mach_20_glider_to_hummingbird_drone.*

CHAPTER EIGHT—WASSIM MATAR: FROM ENGINEER TO VENTURE CAPITALIST

TEDx Talks. "Six keys to leading positive change: Rosabeth Moss Kanter at TEDxBeaconStreet." January 7, 2013. Video, 17:35. *https://youtu.be/owU5aTNPJbs.*

CHAPTER NINE—LINDSEY LYNES: FROM COORDINATOR TO CLIENT SERVICES EXECUTIVE

Anderson, Kare. "Be an opportunity maker." Filmed September 25, 2014 at TED@IBM, San Francisco, CA. Video, 9:36. *https://www.ted.com/talks/kare_anderson_be_an_opportunity_maker.*

CHAPTER TEN—CARTER HOLLAND: FROM GUITARIST TO CORPORATE MARKETER

TEDx Talks. "Everything I know about business I learned from being in a band: Jeb Banner at TEDxIndianapolis." November 17, 2013. Video, 10:08. *https://youtu.be/ZcSLV8agG64.*

CHAPTER ELEVEN—MICHELLE UDEZUE: FROM ACCOUNTANT TO BRAND MARKETER

National Center for Education Statistics, Continuation of Education, Postsecondary Education, Undergraduate Degree Fields. Accessed June 26, 2021. *https://nces.ed.gov/programs/coe/indicator/cta?tid=74.*

CHAPTER TWELVE—EJIEME EROMOSELE: FROM EXPERIENCE CONSULTANT TO CUSTOMER SUCCESS EXECUTIVE

Jacobs, Mia. "What's The Difference Between Customer Success And Customer Experience?". *Totango* (blog). April 8, 2020. *https://blog.totango.com/2020/04/whats-the-difference-between-customer-success-and-customer-experience-fc/.*

TEDx Talks. "Everyday Serendipity | Paul Hannam | TEDxUniversityofBrighton." April 19, 2016. Video, 11:09. *https://youtu.be/xTgKS2bOlqI.*

The New York Times. "Our Path Forward." October 7, 2015. *https://nytco-assets.nytimes.com/m/Our-Path-Forward.pdf.*

CHAPTER THIRTEEN—ANA MARIA GOMEZ LOPEZ: FROM FINANCIAL SERVICES EXECUTIVE TO FINANCIAL TECHNOLOGY EXECUTIVE

Arnold, John D., Chad H. Van Iddekinge, Michael C. Campion, Talya N. Bauer, and Michael A. Campion. "Should You Rehire an Employee Who Left Your Company?" *Harvard Business Review*, February 2, 2021. *https://hbr.org/2021/02/should-you-rehire-an-employee-who-left-your-company.*

CHAPTER FOURTEEN—JONATHAN GODBOUT: FROM GOVERNMENT CONSULTANT TO SOCIAL IMPACT EXECUTIVE

Torres, Roselinde. "What is takes to be a good leader." Filmed October 2013 at TED@BCG San Francisco, San Francisco, CA. Video, 15:26. *https://www.ted.com/talks/.https://www.ted.com/talks/roselinde_torres_what_it_takes_to_be_a_great_leader.*

CHAPTER FIFTEEN—PERSONAL BRAND

Daskal, Lolly. "10 Powerful Ways You Can Earn Credibility in Your Industry." *Lead* (blog). Inc.com. June 13, 2017. *https://www.inc.com/lolly-daskal/10-powerful-ways-you-can-earn-credibility-in-your-industry.html.*

George Washington University. "GWebinar: Making LinkedIn Truly Work for You." August 2015. Video, 1:01:56. *https://gwu.adobeconnect.com/_a948849616/p7jx09fxttz/.*

Jackson, Alice. "8 Reasons Why Business Cards Are Still Important." *Designhill Blog.* February 13, 2019. *https://www.designhill.com/design-blog/reasons-why-business-cards-are-still-important/.*

MIT Sloan Alumni. "Making LinkedIn Work for You – featuring Asha Aravindakshan," SF '17." April 8, 2020. Video, 19:33. *https://youtu.be/QXQ1UMapqyc.*

Preston-Loeb, Karen. "The Importance of Carrying a Business Card." *Furia Rubel* (blog). June 2017. *https://www.furiarubel.com/what-were-up-to/importance-carrying-business-card/.*

Wood, Lottie. "5 Benefits to Having a Business Card." *Lottie Woods Design* (blog). January 29, 2020. *https://www.lottiewoodsdesign. com/blog/5-top-benefits-to-having-a-business-card.*

CHAPTER SIXTEEN—DIGITAL TOOLS

Aaronson, Stephanie and Wendy Edelberg, "Tracking the mounting challenges among those who have lost their jobs." *Upfront* (blog). Brookings Institute, November 5, 2020. *https://www. brookings.edu/blog/up-front/2020/11/05/tracking-the-mounting-challenges-among-those-who-have-lost-their-jobs/.*

Forbes Agency Council. "Is The Business Card Dead? 16 Experts Share Their Thoughts." *Forbes Agency Council* (blog). *Forbes.* November 24, 2017. *https://www.forbes.com/sites/forbesagency-council/2017/11/24/is-the-business-card-dead-16-experts-share-their-thoughts/.*

Monster. "Future of Work 2021 Global Outlook Special Report." *Recruiting Blog* (blog). December 8, 2020. *https://hiring.monster. com/employer-resources/blog/labor-statistics/future-of-work-2021-summary/.*

CHAPTER SEVENTEEN—BUSINESS NETWORKING

Sylvester, Rachel. "Things No One Tells You About Volunteering." *Real Simple.* December 2020.

Tepper, Al. "How To Get Noticed On LinkedIn." Pharus Consulting & TepFu Limited. Streamed live on January 26, 2021. Zoom.

The Meredith Vieira Show. "Nicole Williams' Top Job Tips and Tricks | The Meredith Vieira Show." January 7, 2015. Video, 1:50. *https://youtu.be/1MUqixyN1To.*

CHAPTER EIGHTEEN—ADVICE TO EMPLOYERS

Aravindakshan, Asha. "From the Alumni Association." *GW Magazine*, Spring 2016. p65. *https://archives.magazine.gwu.edu/sites/g/files/zaxdzs1136/f/downloads/GWMag_Spring16_Book_Final-LOWRES.pdf.*

MIT Sloan School of Management. *Career Development Office Year in Review.* February 2021. *https://issuu.com/mitsloancdo/docs/cdo_year_in_review_for_2020?fr=sODYoZTIzNjIzNjE.*

CHAPTER NINETEEN—GUIDE TO YOUR LINKEDIN PROFILE

Anwesha, Jalan, "LinkedIn Profile Photo Tips: Introducing Photo Filters and Editing." *LinkedIn Official Blog.* March 14, 2017. *https://blog.linkedin.com/2017/march/14/linkedin-profile-photo-tips-introducing-photo-filters-and-editing.*

LinkedIn. "College Student Profile Checklist." Higher Education. Accessed May 25, 2021. *https://university.linkedin.com/content/dam/university/global/en_US/site/pdf/LinkedIn%20Profile%20Checklist%20-%20College%20Students.pdf.*

LinkedIn. "High School Student Profile Checklist." Higher Education. Accessed May 25, 2021. *https://university.linkedin.com/content/dam/university/global/en_US/site/pdf/LinkedIn%20Profile%20Checklist%20-%20High%20School%20Students.pdf.*

LinkedIn. "How to Interpret Social Selling Index." Accessed July 26, 2021. *https://business.linkedin.com/sales-solutions/learning-center/resources/tip-sheets/ts022.*

LinkedIn. "LinkedIn Profile Checklist." Premium Resources. Accessed May 25, 2021. *https://premium.linkedin.com/content/premium/global/en_us/index/jobsearch/resources/get-noticed/linkedin-profile-checklist.*

Singer, Natasha. "New Item on the College Admission Checklist: LinkedIn Profile." *The New York Times.* November 5, 2016. *https://www.nytimes.com/2016/11/06/technology/new-item-on-the-college-admission-checklist-linkedin-profile.html.*

THNKR. "6 Elevator Pitches for the 21st Century." February 8, 2013. Video, 4:45. *https://youtu.be/XvxtC6oV6kc.*

TEDx Talks. "LinkedIn's Community: A Superpower Hiding in Plain Sight | Sandra Long | TEDxFergusonLibrary." May 29, 2019. Video, 11:39. *https://youtu.be/uwWRArh8wAY.*

CONCLUSION

Oberlin College. "Martin Luther King, Jr. at Oberlin." *Oberlin College Archives.* Last modified February, 11, 2009. *https://www2.oberlin.edu/external/EOG/BlackHistoryMonth/MLK/KingAutograph.html.*

Schein, Edgar H. and John Van Maanen. "Career anchors and job/role planning: Tools for career and talent management." *Organizational Dynamics*, Volume 45, Issue 3, 2016, Pages 165-173, ISSN 0090-2616, *https://doi.org/10.1016/j.orgdyn.2016.07.002.*

Trunk, Penelope. "Make Life More Stable with More Frequent Job Changes." *[...PT...]* (blog). February 25, 2007. *https://blog.penelopetrunk.com/2007/02/25/make-your-life-more-stable-by-changing-jobs-more-frequently/.*

Whiting, Kate. "These are the top 10 job skills of tomorrow – and how long it takes to learn them." *Global Agenda* (blog) . World Economic Forum. October 21, 2020. *https://www.weforum.org/agenda/2020/10/top-10-work-skills-of-tomorrow-how-long-it-takes-to-learn-them/.*

Made in the USA
Middletown, DE
11 October 2021

49842187R00157